Black
to
BLUE

JAMIE ROONEY

Black to BLUE

© 2016 Jamie Rooney.

Print ISBN: 978-1-68222-846-3

eBook ISBN: 978-1-68222-847-0

I dedicate this book to my beautiful children who remind me every day just how precious life is.

Acknowledgments

I would not have been able to share my story without the constant support and encouragement of my dear friends Joanne Terrasi and Frank Wallace. I am deeply grateful for your unwavering faith in my ability to share so many personal pieces of my life. I would also like to thank my incredibly talented editor Mark Chimsky. Mark helped to mold my story, giving it form and fluency. Joanne, Frank and Mark helped me to become a writer. Thanks to them I was able to bring my experiences to life.

The second most important person in this book is my sister Marie. She tolerated several phone calls involving me triple checking my facts for consistency and accuracy. This book holds a piece of her story. I am blessed that she allowed me to share portions of her past with my readers.

I can't go further without thanking my York Police Department Family. I believe it is a gift to my life that I am able to do what I do. I love my place in this crazy world of Law Enforcement. I would not be here if it were not for their solid support and trust.

"My mission in life is not merely to survive, but to thrive; and to do so with some passion, some compassion, some humor, and some style."

- **Maya Angelou**

"We can let the circumstances of our lives harden us so that we become increasingly resentful and afraid, or we can let them soften us, and make us kinder. You always have a choice."

- **Dalai Lama**

I have changed the names of the characters in this book to protect their privacy. This is my opportunity to tell my story, from my perspective. The content is mature and difficult to read at certain points. I strongly recommend parents read the book before giving it to young adults. A parent is the only person that can know if their child will be able to handle the material.

Main Characters

Jack - my son

Riley - my daughter

Lori - my mother

Marie - older sister (same parents)

Andrew - younger half brother (different fathers, same mother)

Jessie - younger half sister (different fathers, same mother)

Dave – Lori's longtime boyfriend (Andrew and Jessie's father)

Michael - younger half brother (same father, different mother)

Doris - my grandmother on my father's side

Aunt Maggie - mother's side

Aunt Peg - mother's side

Uncle Charles - mother's side

Aunt Sam - Uncle Charles's wife

Deborah (aka "Red") - stepmother, father's third wife

Aunt Mary - father side

Uncle Paul - father's side

Rick – Red's son

Chris – Red's oldest son

Samantha - neighbor and long time friend

Jane & Jim - Samantha's parents

Introduction

As an officer I have the ability to impact lives on a daily basis. I am so very fortunate that my path has brought me here. I am the Resource and Drug Abuse Resistance Education (DARE) Officer for a beautiful community in York, Maine.

This book is my opportunity to show those who are struggling with difficult times that they do not have to be a victim no matter how terrible their circumstances are. I grew up in the projects. I spent most of my childhood looking for food and clothing in order to survive. I was surrounded by drugs and alcohol my entire childhood. I bought drugs for my mother. I also was the victim of physical and sexual abuse as I grew up. My journey was one filled with pain and suffering but every day I knew one day I would get away from it all and live my own life. I feel so very blessed to have the opportunity to share my story. My life has been a challenge but I would not change it for anything in this world because every experience made me who I am today. My students at the York Middle School tell me that that I am "the coolest cop ever." Now that makes it all worth it.

Before I talk about my career in law enforcement I should show you how it all began. " Buckle up," it's one hell of a ride.

Grab your flip-flop. I want the green one. I'm going to kick your ass this time! Ok, now when I turn the light on we will see who the champion is. I held the record for the most roaches killed with a flip flop at 18 kills. Marie was desperate to steal my title. The lights were off for about 20 minutes. You wanted the roaches to have a false sense of security. Let them think it's their time to come out. Little did they know we were patiently standing outside the door planning our attack. Start low and work your way up. They would be scattering desperately to reach the seams down by the floor. Ready, set and GO... Laughter filled the air as we raced one another. Constantly looking over our shoulders, checking the others' progress. These nasty little insects came in all sizes. Some were as large as my thumb and others as small as the tip of a marker. The large roaches cracked when you smashed them. You could feel the snap of their shell. If I were to tell my children today about this game I am confident they would think I was making it up. With their I Pads, Xbox games, Duct Tape purses, and every craft kit known to man at their fingertips, my children have never had to worry about bugs crawling on them in their sleep.

We didn't make purses with Duct Tape in the projects. We had practical uses for it. You would place it so that the sticky part was facing up and put a small piece of bread in the middle. On a good night, you would catch at least 20 roaches. Looking back, I believe this flip-flop game was about revenge. It allowed us to take back control and to help us to fight the fear of roaches crawling on our bodies, in our hair, and even worse -- in our mouths. We scared them. Then, killed them.

What does a six-year-old little peanut know about survival? You would be surprised.

My oldest memories as a child are of situations and circumstances that required survival

skills. When I think about some of the situations I put myself in, I am amazed that I am

alive, never mind working to protect and serve. This is my story.

1

Precious Years: 1983 - 1990

I was six years old when we moved to Great Brook Valley in Worcester, Massachusetts. That was the name of the projects we lived in, Great Brook Valley. We called it the Valley for short. There were rows and rows of three-story brick apartment buildings with six apartments in each section. We lived at 15B, building 15, apartment B. It was a two-bedroom apartment. Our front yard consisted of cement landings and pavement. Each building had a cement stoop with just a few steps leading up to a cement landing at the entrance. There wasn't enough room for a chair or a potted plant, just enough to get yourself up into the building. A large, green-metal door with a broken lock was propped open with a heavy cement brick to allow easy access. Outside of our building, just about ten feet from our front doorway was a large fenced-in area with clotheslines running throughout. It was large enough for five buildings to share. Just beyond the clotheslines, you came to a parking area and two dumpsters. In the same direction, across the main street that ran the length of the projects, was the city bus stop. The bus was the only mode of transportation other than our legs during my six years in the projects. The set-up was very practical. The projects' management made sure that we had everything and anything we would ever need.

I would dream of a grass-covered yard to run through with my bare feet. What I would have given to roll down a grassy hill so fast that it would make me want to throw up. Worcester is not the place to roll down hills, even if they are covered in grass. There was broken glass and garbage spread everywhere you looked. Some of the blocks further down the road had wooden landings with a couple of shrubs and a few sprigs of

10

grass. We had only pavement, but we learned how to make the most of everything. Pavement was great for hopscotch, jump rope, and skateboarding; three of my favorite things to do growing up. Behind the block of buildings was a playground area. The roadway running between our buildings and another set behind us had been turned into basketball courts, swing sets, and slides. They were simple and to the point but, nonetheless, they were for kids, at least during the daytime. We knew not to hang out there past eight at night. Too many bad things could happen to you after eight. It was no secret the streets were overrun with drugs and violence. Newsworthy shootings and beatings happened every few months. We might have owned the Valley during the day but we feared it during the night.

At first there were five of us in the two-bedroom apartment: my mother, Lori; her boyfriend, Dave; my older sister, Marie; and my baby brother, Andrew. I had a younger sister, Jessie, but her arrival was about a year after the move. Altogether, my mother had four children. Two sets by two different men. She met my father when she was 18 or 19. She met Dave when she was around 22 years old. There have been many men in her life but these two men were the only two that ever really mattered.

The walls were paper-thin. We were on the bottom floor and with that came nonstop entertainment from our neighbors. Doors slamming, yelling and fighting, dancing and, of course, I can't fail to mention Lori's lovemaking. I learned early in life what that sounded like and even looked like. When you have so many people living in a small apartment you tend to walk in on things no child should ever have to witness. I knew enough not to ask questions and to walk right back out of the room. Some things you just never talked about and that was most definitely one of them.

My childhood molded me. My experiences taught me so many important lessons. We all learn how to fly but how well we fly depends on how well we learn. Fortunately I knew when to pay attention. I also refused to give up. I could tell myself when something was messed up. I knew what I wanted for my life and my future family. I promised myself many times that I would not make choices that would harm my future, The circumstances and situations that I am about to share led me on a path to law enforcement. I had to make difficult choices along the way but nevertheless I made them. Let me fill in some of the blanks.

2

Life in the Projects

Great Brook Valley. The name was confusing to me. There was nothing great about the projects. The apartments were infested with roaches and people were stacked on top of each other. A two-bedroom apartment usually housed four to six people. The kitchen was a hallway that could only fit two people at a time, standing side by side. The washing machine was pushed up against the window in the kitchen 3 feet from the door. We had just enough room to open the front door. The walls were painted chalk-white with primer paint. There were certain rules set by the Valley and you could be fined for not following them. You were not allowed to paint the inside of your apartment. Or put nails in the walls. This made hanging pictures difficult. We didn't have anything to hang anyhow. Some people would hang tapestries with thumbtacks to add some color. They were more ambitious than Lori. We had cheap, plastic, white blinds on our windows in the living room and bed sheets covered our bedroom windows. Mattresses lined the floor and you were fortunate if you had both a sheet *and* a blanket. Pillows were rolled-up old clothes stuffed in a pillowcase or old sweatshirts with the arms tied. Everything smelled the same. The smell of cigarette smoke filled our home, clothes, bedding, and hair. You get the idea.

Our apartment was never quiet or peaceful. No cookies or muffins being baked in the oven. If you did want to use the oven, you would have to prepare yourself for the roaches that came crawling out of all of the seams trying to escape the heat. Lori never used the oven. On special occasions she would boil chicken legs and make powdered mashed potatoes. Those were the special nights, like Easter or Thanksgiving. For Christmas, if we were lucky, we would have a canned ham. I was not a fan of the jelly that came with the ham when you popped it out of the can. I really wasn't a fan of the ham either, but you can put mustard on anything and make it taste good

Drugs were a normal part of our everyday life. We didn't know any different. I wouldn't think twice about a mirror on the kitchen table covered in cocaine dust with a couple of cut-up straws lying near by, waiting to be used. Lori and her friends smoked marijuana daily. It was considered acceptable and along the same lines as cigarettes. I can't tell you how many times I was passed a joint because the person handing it didn't realize that I was a child standing by watching. I would just continue to pass it along without hesitation. This was our way of life. This was normal. This was life in the projects.

The Valley was a community of people living in poor conditions with poor circumstances just trying to make it through the day. As a community we stuck together and we handled our own shit. I would invite friends over and not be the least bit concerned that they would see the drugs and go and tell on my mother. I didn't have to worry about that because either their home was the same way or we trusted the code of the projects. No one wanted to be a rat and no one went to the police. Those who lived in the projects you handled your problems with a good ass-kicking followed by a "Don't ever fuck with me again." That usually took care of any issues. I knew how to fight at a very young age.

My life was about survival. Getting by in the most basic way; like knowing where to go for free food and clothing and how to stand up to others who may try to hurt my family or me. Even as a young child I knew what to say and do to get the most I could. I knew how to protect my family from being a target. I understood human nature and psychology even as a six-year-old little girl. I knew how to manipulate my situations by realizing the bigger picture and knowing what I wanted for an end result. I found myself five steps ahead of the other kids around me. I could read the body language of the people around me. I watched how people looked at my friends and me. I was different. I stood out. This was crystal clear to all of us. I knew when it was time to hit the bricks, as we would call it. I understood that most people had agendas. If I thought their agenda was going to put me in a bad situation I would "hit the bricks." If I thought I could benefit from a certain situation I would stick around and use charm. Every situation was different. Most times I would stick around. I usually ended up with a free warm meal at one of my friend's homes. I made friends very easily but I did not trust anyone. This was a curse and a blessing. It was a curse because I couldn't keep myself from analyzing everything. It was a blessing because it helped me survive circumstances and situations that would have crushed many adults.

I didn't find myself scared too often. The one thing that did scare me was men. The way they looked at me. Their slow-moving eyes going up and down my small figure. The hairs on the back of my neck would stand straight up. Then there was the way they talked to me. I knew what they were thinking and I knew what they wanted. I also knew enough to not be alone in a room with them and to always travel with someone with me. No place was safe. Day or night, it didn't matter.

15

One hot summer day, I walked about a mile to my friend's building to see if she could come out and play. I could feel someone behind me. I felt a terrible uneasiness in the pit of my stomach but I didn't know what that feeling even meant. My brain was telling my body that this person was up to something and I needed to get away from him as fast as I could. My inner voice was speaking to me but I was too young to listen.

I looked back and he acted as if he was just walking and so I continued. He had to have been following me for a while, getting closer and closer as we went along. When I looked back he was still far enough behind me, so I wasn't too worried, as I got to the building where my friend lived, and I walked up the stairs, he was right behind me. The next thing I knew he had followed me into the building and was pinning me up in the corner on the first floor. He had closed the heavy hallway door behind him so it was dark. Though the indoor lighting was very poor, I could see him. His arms were braced against the walls on each side of me. He was tall and heavyset. I had seen him outside earlier in the day playing basketball with a group of men. I noticed him because of the way he watched me. He also stood out because he was white, and there were not many white people in the projects. He was in his early twenties with blonde hair and blue eyes. He wore a white jumpsuit that didn't look good on him. The suit was cheep and too tight around his waist.

I was nine years old at the time. "You're very pretty," he said as he leaned into me. His eyes scared me. I knew what he was thinking. He was very confident, as if his compliment meant something special to me. He touched my hair and ran his fingers through it. I wanted to spit in his face but I stayed calm while I tried to think of a plan. I needed to escape but there was no way around him and everything was happening so fast. He then grabbed my hand and put it on his hard penis. He looked into my eyes and said, "Do you know what that is?"

I pulled my hand back quickly. I didn't speak a word. I was so scared. There was no way out. I knew I was screwed. If I hit this guy he would crush me with one hand. Suddenly, the door cracked open and I was saved by a little brown girl. I can see her face now. She had no idea what she walked into. The door opened and light beamed through the hallway. Looking back I am sure the girl saw the terror on my face. I remember she had a mushroom haircut and a tiny nose. She seemed very surprised. The man stepped back with fear, not seeing who had opened the door and I quickly ducked under his arm and ran out the door. I continued running until I was home. I have no idea what happened to that little girl. When I got home, I stood outside my door, and took a moment to catch my breath. Then, I walked in as if nothing had happened. I went into my room, put my head down on my desk in front of my radio, and turned the music up loud enough to get rid of the thoughts in my head. I sat there for at least two hours.

I never told anyone about the guy or what had happened and I never went back to that apartment building alone again. The man didn't go away. He lived in the projects. I knew this because every once in a while I would see him outside playing hoops or standing with a group of guys. He would watch me walk by and I could feel his eyes. I never looked his way and I never stopped walking. Part of me wanted to flip him off but I knew it would force an interaction that I would lose. So, I would walk by him fast and get the hell out of there. I was always prepared to run if he took one step in my direction. He never did. He just stood there staring.

The backside of the building facing the play area also had back hallways into our buildings. We only used these hallways as a last resort. It was worth your time to leave from the front hallway and avoid anyone that may be in the back. Needles littered the back hallways. The smell of piss was pungent. The sight of a sad soul propped up in a corner staring off, or even worse, staring at you, was enough to scare a little girl shitless. I avoided the back hallways. Most people had metal bars across their back doors for extra security. The front hallways were clean for the most part. When people came to your home you wanted it to look presentable. People had little "Welcome" signs on the doors or small mats with "Home Sweet Home" written across it. But those things provided nothing more than a false sense of security for all of us. We stuck to the front hallways. The few times I did take the back hallway I learned my lesson quickly.

I have a "one and done" rule that I've followed since I was a child. I have a lot of rules but this one is crucial for survival. If something really scary or dangerous happens to you and you manage to make it out reasonably unharmed, you can never allow yourself to make that mistake again. I intentionally took the back hallway as a shortcut one day and I never did that again. It was the middle of the day and I didn't really care that people had warned me to avoid it. I walked up the front stairs and the door closed behind me. As I turned the corner, I could see that there was a white coffee cup at the top of the steps just above our door. I could see two or three needles sticking out of it. About a foot from the cup was the sole of a shoe. I said, "Hello," but no one answered. The person on the floor above me didn't move. I couldn't tell if it was a man or woman. The shoe was a tennis-type of shoe. It was large enough to belong to a male but not too large and so it could have been a woman. I said, "Hello, are you ok?" but there was still no answer.

I thought that maybe someone had fallen down the stairs and that they were hurt or worse. I looked at the cup and thought it was too far away from this person to have just been used. I convinced myself that everything was fine, but I just had to check. I couldn't stop myself. I slowly walked halfway up the stairs. There were nine steps. I could see an arm and the side of a person. They had hard, weathered skin. I said "hello" again and still no reply. My heart was beating and I was sad for this poor person in my hallway. I made it to the eighth step and finally I could see his face. He was alive and breathing funny. He was looking at me but I don't think he could see me. There was no reaction to my presence. Suddenly, I was scared. Before I had just been worried, but now I was scared. Things started to add up. There was a needle lying next to his leg. I knew that was his needle because of the thing wrapped around his other arm. I ran down the stairs and back outside. I didn't stop at my door. It would take my mother too long to unlock it, if she was even home. I ran outside and then back around to the front. I learned my lesson and I swore I would never take that back hallway again.

Living in the Valley I was accustomed to strangers always being in our apartment for late-night parties that typically resulted in people I had never met passing out on our floor. Oftentimes they would piss themselves and you could smell their pungent urine, as they laid unconscious in it. Morning would come and I found myself walking around them to get out the door so that I wouldn't be late for school. The leftover dust remnants of coke on the table was just another sight as I headed out. That along with the party bowl in the kitchen sink that was completely empty and the marijuana seeds piled off to the side where Lori had been rolling her bones. If she had a large bag, she would let me and my older sister Marie pick the seeds out for her. We thought this was fun. Looking back, I'm amazed that I didn't grow up to be a pothead too.

As I made my way to the door, tiptoeing around the passed-out fools on my floor, I would occasionally check their pockets for cash. I justified my actions by telling myself they were in *my* apartment, on *my* floor. They didn't care that they had kept us up most of the night so I didn't care that I took their money. I will be honest. I didn't just do it once in a while, I did it every time. I knew I would have to eat at some point and a buck or two would buy me a donut or a Little Debbie on my way to school. I can't believe that no one ever woke up while I was checking their pockets. I had a system down, I guess. I was quiet and clever but still you would think at least one person would have been startled awake as I rummaged through their pockets. If they had I am sure that I would have come up with some kind of explanation.

My biggest score was 36 dollars off of this blond, scrawny woman who desperately needed to eat something. She looked like a walking skeleton. I took the money out of her tacky blue patent-leather purse that had a big gold buckle. I thought to myself, *Who in the world would buy this purse?* It's funny to think I had any kind of fashion sense back then. The ugly purse did not stop me from taking her money. I ran outside with the cash and took it around to the side of the building where I would be hidden. I counted the money three times to make sure that I had it right. I was nervous because it was so much cash and I knew I would probably get caught with it. I decided I would do what they do on television and bury it in a coffee can, but first I was running late so I hid it in a crack in the bricks. I figured that when I came home I could find a can and dig a hole. It would be my buried treasure.

That day at school couldn't go by fast enough! All I could think about was that money and what I was going to do with my big payday. When I got home the money was right where I left it. I found a coffee can in the closet that was perfect for my treasure, and I kept it buried for two whole days. That was the longest I could go without seeing it. It was without a doubt burning a hole in my pocket. I spent the money on a package of socks and underwear. The underwear was the kind that had the days of the week on them. I had always wanted those but we couldn't afford them. Now, I finally had some. I also bought a few pieces of candy and a large jar of pickles. I loved pickles. The dill kind. Lori would never buy them so I went out and bought my own. I hid the jar in my room and ate every single one. Lori never asked me about the money either. I doubt the woman even realized it was gone. Lori didn't notice my awesome new underwear either. My daughter wears the same kind now and every time I fold a pair I get a little chuckle out of remembering how I got my first pair.

There were so many occasions of drug use in our house but one stands out more than any other. It was late and I was sitting on the couch in the living room. I watched as Lori sat at the card table with a man with a black moustache, whom I had never seen before, and a small-framed Hispanic woman. The table was pressed up against the sidewall to save space. The couch I was on was about two feet from them. I was watching some show on our little 19-inch television. I can't recall for sure if we had cable but I think we did. Anyhow, the three adults were snorting lines of coke. I watched as they divided it up. They chopped it up into a fine dust with a straight-edged razor and then took a straw and cut it short. This was one of those defining moments people talk about. I will never forget it.

The Hispanic woman looked at me as if she had just noticed that I was there. She stopped what she was doing and stared for what felt like forever. I stared right back, not changing the expression on my face. Then, as if she suddenly had a conscience, she said to my mother, "We shouldn't be doing this in front of your daughter."

The response was priceless. Lori just shrugged her shoulders and without missing a beat she said, "I don't hide anything from my kids."
This did not surprise me. It was her out. Sounding as if she was being a good mother by being honest and upfront. She didn't hesitate to then take the straw and do her line. I shrugged my shoulders and went back to watching my show. I knew that my mother

was screwed up. I knew that this was wrong but, again, this was all that I knew. This was my reality and she was my mom. It took a lot for Lori to surprise me. Nothing was too far out for her. You just had to roll with the punches. What choice did we really have?

The words I hated to hear more than anything were, "Can you do me a favor?" Lori would ask me to walk a few blocks away to a certain "friend" of hers and pick up a joint or "bone" (as she called them) for her. She would put the rolled-up cash into my hand. She had shown me how to carry the joint so that I wouldn't bend or break it. I would wear a long-sleeved shirt and tuck the joint up into my sleeve. I walked back with my arm straight, being extremely careful not to harm my mother's joint. The first time I did this I was scared but after a couple of times I got comfortable with it and it didn't bother me. I would walk to the apartment she told me to go to, and knock on the door. A Hispanic man would answer the door. I told him my mother had sent me and I would hand him the rolled-up bills. He would hand me the joint cupped in his hand. I would tuck it in my sleeve and then be on my way. Thankfully, this was the only type of drug she ever allowed me to get for her. I never asked her why she couldn't go and get it herself. After all, I had watched my half-brother Andrew and half-sister Jessie on so many occasions. She could have gone anytime. That was never an issue. There had to have been some reason why she would have her young daughter walk two blocks away, sometimes farther, just to buy her a joint when she was more than capable of doing this herself. The part that absolutely kills me is that she was never worried about me getting hurt. She was perfectly fine with sending me to a drug dealer's house so that she could have a quick buzz. At the time I wasn't angry. I was definitely annoyed but never angry. As an adult with children of my own, the more I think about this the angrier I get.

I remember a time I was leaving my friend Anna's apartment and as I walked down the stairs I found a baggie of coke on top of the hallway light cover. It was placed just enough on the side so that I could see the top of the baggy. I am sure someone was on their way to get it. I knew instantly that if I was going to take it, I had better do it fast. I threw the baggy up into my sleeve and booked it out of that hallway. I ran all the way home to give it to Lori as if I were bringing her a gift. She was extremely happy when I presented it to her. I don't know why I didn't throw it away or just leave it alone. I knew this would be a fantastic surprise. She bragged to a couple of her girlfriends about my find and they were thrilled for my mother. This seemed to give me a sense of pride in a strange way.

I hated drugs then and yet I delivered them to my mother to make her happy. I'm not really sure how I feel about this now. The only thing I know is that every child wants to please their parent no matter how messed up they are. I was no different. I wanted her to be happy and Lori was only happy when she had her beer and drugs. It was also an opportunity for me to get her attention. I wanted my mother to love me. I wanted my mother to kiss me on the head and hug me when I was scared. I wanted my mother to tuck me in at night. I wanted my mother to notice me. On this day, she noticed me.

I had an incredible amount of freedom living with Lori in the projects. I came and went as I pleased. She never asked for check-ins or phone numbers of my friends' parents. I did what I wanted when I wanted. I would take the city bus once a week into the center of town with friends to walk around the Galleria Mall. This was right behind city hall in Worcester. It cost 35 cents to ride the bus one way back then. I would find the money anywhere I could in order to get to the mall. When it was time to come home I would reach my hand into the wishing fountain in the center of the mall and take out what I needed to get back. My system never failed me. Worst case, I would ask some woman that looked like a mother for change to get home. I have to say I was darn cute and they couldn't resist me. At least that is what I told myself. I never stole at the mall. I knew that the chances of getting caught there were much higher than at your average department store. The security officers were always walking around. I knew enough not to push my luck.

Going to the Galleria was my opportunity to be around pretty things and people-watch. I loved seeing all the different types of people walk by. I would pretend that I was wealthy and I could have whatever it was that I wanted. I would stop in front of shop windows and stare at the outfits as if I had a choice to purchase one. I loved to fantasize that my life was different, that I wasn't poor. The Galleria was the perfect place for this escape. I would always have a friend or two with me. It's funny thinking back now how we were never asked where our parents were. No one ever seemed concerned that little kids were riding the bus alone into downtown Worcester, or roaming the mall for hours. When I got home, which was usually around dusk, Lori wouldn't ask where I had been and I wouldn't offer any explanation to her.

3

Lori

She was born in 1957 in Worcester, Massachusetts. She was the third of five children. She had one older sister, an older brother, and a younger sister and brother born just a couple years after her. Her father died when she was a child. Her mother, Marianne, worked long days in a factory in Worcester to try to support her five children. I am not sure what type of work she did but I know she also spent her share of time at the local pub. Overwhelmed with being a young widow with five kids, Marianne turned to alcohol for comfort. She had married the love of her life and was devastated when she lost him. She never married again.

The oldest of the children, Charles, took on the role of parent and disciplinarian. From what I have learned over the years, Charles was a violent and cruel man. He beat his siblings on a regular basis; pulling their hair and punching them in the face. Basically, he did what he wanted, when he wanted, because no one was there to stop him. I once heard that "Uncle Charles" went to jail for beating his girlfriend to a bloody pulp, after putting a dog collar on her and forcing her to eat dog food out of the dog's bowl. Like I said, he was cruel. Lori told me about how hard Uncle Charles was on her. She said he would beat the shit out of her just for fun. She was a very skinny young woman and she had no strength to protect herself. He would laugh as she cried. I never felt comfortable around him. Something inside my gut told me to beware. I never allowed myself to get too close to him. I was close with his first wife, Sam. She was an incredible woman -- extremely kind and loving -- without a mean bone in her body. How she ended up with him I have no clue. He didn't deserve her. Last I heard, Uncle Charles had become a heroin addict, living in and out of shelters. I hope he has found happiness in his life. I hope that he has found a way to live a healthier life. I will never have a relationship with him. He is not someone I would allow to be around my children. That being said, I do hope he is doing better for himself and his family.

For me, it's important to see where Lori came from in order to fully understand how her life turned out the way it did. Lori dropped out of school in eighth grade and she never went back. She never got a driver's license or worked any particular job for any length of time. I am still not sure if she had learning disabilities or if she just struggled emotionally. I tend to think she really didn't care and decided not to do anything that she didn't have to do.

I was told that before I was born, Lori worked in the factories like her mother but I have no memory of her working. Kids were her ticket to welfare and welfare was her ticket to never having to work again. She never talked about dreams or ambitions. I don't think I ever saw her pick up a book or even a magazine for that matter. She was, however, a social butterfly. She could talk to anyone. She had a calm and friendly voice, definitely feminine and easy to warm up to. If she were semi-sober, she could be friendly and fun to talk to. She loved to gossip with the other moms in the projects as they sat outside in their plastic lawn chairs working on their tans. They would sit all day with their baby oil, smoking their cigarettes and drinking cheap beer.

When she drank all day, her demons would come out at night. It was like a witching hour hit and you had better watch out. You did not want to piss her off and it was best to just stay out of her way. Even her facial features seemed to change. She looked like a different person when she was shit-faced. I figured out very quickly when to stick around and when to "get out of Dodge."

Lori had long beautiful legs. They were her trademarks. People always commented on my mother's long, brown hair and her long, lean legs. She loved that. She had a small frame with curves in the right places. She wore makeup every day and wouldn't leave the house without it. I hated the way it looked on her skin and I hated the way it felt on mine when she hugged me; somehow, she would always get liquid foundation on me. Lori had severe acne as a young woman and she tried to cover her pock-marked skin. She loved her mascara as much as she loved her liquid makeup. Her eyes are crystal blue and the mascara did make them pop. I told her that many times. The mascara I could live with but the liquid makeup had to go.

She was attractive in a simple way. Men looked as she walked by and usually commented on her. She always wore cut-off short-shorts, making sure to show off those perfect legs and tight rear. I didn't understand how she managed it. She never worked out a day in her life. She abused her body day and night. It did eventually catch up with her but back then she had something to be shown.

From what I can tell, Lori was an alcoholic probably since the time when her father died. The drugs came along later in life. I was told by her longtime boyfriend Dave, that she was using when they met, so I was just a newborn. He told me how they used heroin together, and that he was thankful that they were both able to stop using. I don't know what it took for that to happen but I am truly grateful for that. I know someone was looking out for us those days. As a mother, I wonder who the hell was taking care of us while all of this was happening and how the hell Lori is even still alive.

Lori's side of the family is Irish through and through and for them, alcohol was as abundant as water. It was "our heritage." My great grandparents were "off the boat." This is what people say when they want to really get the point that they are IRISH! My great grandmother was absolutely adorable. She was a petite little lady with the Irish accent and all. I never saw her drink a drop of alcohol. Lori and her siblings used their heritage as an excuse to get shitfaced and spend hours at the local Irish pub, especially around St. Patrick's Day. Before the Valley, when we lived in town, my older sister Marie and I went to the bar several times with Lori. We knew the bartenders by name and they were always nice to us. I would get a root beer. Marie would get a Shirley Temple. While my mother socialized with her bar friends we would play games together or with the bartender. He would bring us pretzels and help us as we worked hard to build our card houses. He always put us into a booth to shelter us from the surroundings. We were the only kids in the bar so we felt special. When it grew dark outside, we would walk home or go upstairs and stay with my Aunt Juliet. The apartment was a two-bedroom unit with a small kitchen and living room. The walls were yellow from all of the tobacco smoke stained on the walls. There was always a pot of coffee on. There were two things Aunt Juliet lived on, Coffee and Cigarettes. She wasn't really my aunt but she and my mother were close. Juliet would look after us often when Dave wasn't around. I have a hard time remembering when Dave was and was not around. At five years old, it wasn't always easy to keep up with that relationship. Once we moved to the Valley, we didn't go to the bar anymore. It was too far to walk, and so the bar came to us.

Among my mother's siblings, Auntie Maggie was our guardian angel. She was older than Lori and definitely more squared away. She had a son named James and we were born the same year. James and I were very close. I was fortunate because I got to be his playmate for special occasions. James was the lucky one. His father George lived in Worcester and so he was able to see him almost every week. He would take James fishing and spend time playing with him. I envied their relationship. One time, when George offered to take Maggie and James to the fair, Aunt Maggie said she would only go if I could come too. George was still in love with her and would do anything she asked. It was a win-win for me: I got to go and I got away from the projects!

Aunt Maggie would come by and straighten my mother out on occasion, especially if Lori went on a "bender" and drank from sunup to sundown. Someone would get ahold of Aunt Maggie and she would hurry over to our place and have a little heart-to-heart with Lori. This always seemed to work.

Aunt Maggie was tall, much taller than me, and she was a scrapper known for kicking ass and taking names. She lived in the projects with James when we first moved in but she found a way out as fast as possible by putting herself through school and getting her LPN. She started working nights in a hospital to pay her bills. We were all really proud of her and I looked up to her. I remember many times when I was feeling low; she would tell me that I could be whatever I wanted to be. She was what real family is supposed to be.

Aunt Maggie also went out of her way to show us her support. When Marie and I had a Christmas concert or the spring fling right before summer vacation, she was always in the crowd, cheering us on. She knew we needed attention that we weren't getting from anyone else and I liked the fact that she didn't try to make excuses for Lori. She would just move past the questions and tell us that she loved us. That was good enough for me. If one of us were sick, she would take care of us. I had an ear infection one year and I still remember it was the worst pain I had ever felt, like an ice pick that was scraping the insides of both ears. Aunt Maggie just happened to stop by and after taking one look at me, we were immediately off to the hospital. It turned out I had a severe double ear infection. The doctor said that he could not believe how long we had let this go. He eased the piercing pain in my ears by giving me special eardrops. My aunt lied for my mother and said that she was really sick and couldn't have known how bad I had been feeling. If my aunt had told the doctor the truth, we both knew that DHS (The Department of Human Services) would get a call and that would not have been good. The ear infection was gone in just a few days. The pain was almost gone by the second or third day.

On the other end of the spectrum was Aunt Peg, my mother's younger sister. Aunt Peg and Lori had a lot in common. They both loved to party. They both raised their children on welfare and they both loved drugs. Aunt Peg was in and out of my life as we grew up. She lived on the other side of town and so we didn't see her much. She didn't have a car or driver's license so in order to get to her house; we would have to take a cab or bus and then walk. She didn't take a real interest in our lives and we didn't take much of an interest in hers either. One summer, when I was 12 years old, Aunt Peg invited me to go on a weekend trip with her, her boyfriend at the time, and her two daughters, who were just a couple of years younger than me. I had been spending more time with them this particular summer and I had no reservations of going with all of them on the trip. We were going camping in the boyfriend's large van, traveling up the coast and hitting beaches along the way.

On the day that changed our relationship forever we were in the Salisbury Beach area. It was the last day of the trip and I was sitting in the back of the van with the two girls. I remember that we had been playing with some Barbie dolls. Aunt Peg and her boyfriend had been partying hard all weekend and Aunt Peg had been drinking all day. Her boyfriend was driving the van. I remember laughing at a story that he was telling me. Suddenly, as if a switch had gone off inside her head, Aunt Peg's expression changed and I knew that something was very wrong. It was the same face that Lori would make when her demons were about to come out.

Aunt Peg climbed out of her seat and crawled into the back of the van. Then she started hitting me, shouting that I was trying to "fuck" her boyfriend. I was in complete shock. I had no idea where this was coming from. I could hear my cousins crying and telling her to stop. I held her back as best I could with my feet and legs, kicking like crazy. She finally stopped and returned to her seat. By that time, her boyfriend had pulled the van over. As Aunt Peg sat and collected herself, I was crying uncontrollably. I felt so betrayed and hurt. Her boyfriend tried to talk sense into her, but she just punched him a few times, asking him if he wanted me. I couldn't believe what I was hearing. None of this made any sense and I couldn't do anything: I was stuck in this van. She came back at me one more time. Thankfully, her boyfriend pulled her off of me. I put as many blankets and pillows in front of me for protection. Less than an hour later, we pulled into a beach parking lot at Salisbury Beach. I had never heard of this place and so I had no way of knowing where I was or how I was going to get home.

Once Aunt Peg grabbed a spot on the beach and passed out, I told everyone that I was going to the bathroom. I went to the closest shop and asked if I could use their phone. The owner was a small woman with brown shoulder length hair. I remember that she had a daughter close to my age and an older son. They had an apartment up above their shop. I told her that my aunt had attacked me and I needed help. She was shocked when she saw the scratches and red marks on my face and arms and quickly called the police. When the dispatcher asked to speak with me, I got on the phone and answered all her questions. I tried to be brave and hold back my tears, and I was glad when I heard her say, "Don't worry, I'll send an officer to help you right away."

The officer arrived shortly after. He came upstairs and met with me while a second officer went to find Peg to tell her that I wasn't going to go with her. I was then taken to the police station and called the one person in this world that I knew would come and get me: Aunt Maggie.

It took my Aunt Maggie a couple of hours to get to us but I didn't mind. I hung out with the officers for a while. They bought me some food and eventually, after I managed to calm down, I fell asleep on the wooden bench in the waiting area. I woke to the sound of Aunt Maggie's voice. She was so kind to me. I told her what had happened and she just hugged me and said that everything was going to be ok. Since that day, I have not had any kind of a relationship with Aunt Peg. She has struggled her entire life with substance abuse. I don't know if my mother ever found forgiveness in her heart for Aunt Peg. I do wish her a happy and a healthy life. I know that her two oldest daughters have worked hard and created great lives for themselves. That makes me very happy.

My mother had had a rough life when she was a young girl, so I understand why she was desperate to find a way out of the family home. Her opportunity came when Aunt Juliet introduced her to my father, who had come down to Massachusetts from Maine for an extended stay after graduating from high school. They were married shortly after they met. My sister Marie was born within that year and two years later I came along. But when I was three months old, my parents were divorced. Lori had caught my father in bed with Marie's babysitter when she was pregnant with me. She packed up Marie and we all went back to Worcester. Even when my mother gave birth to me soon after, it wasn't enough to heal her broken heart. She had lost the man who had been her knight. She swore she would never marry again and she kept that promise.

My parents always remained civil to one another. As far back as I can remember, they never spoke badly about one another. They would respect each other's opinions about what was best for us. My mother had every opportunity to tell us how terrible our father was -- how he had slept with Marie's sitter and broke up their marriage -- but she never did. We found out the full story as we got older and he never denied it. I believe my father was just happy that we were with our mother when we were young. He was definitely not interested in being a single dad. I am extremely grateful that they never put us in the middle of their garbage. There was no trash-talking and we were never forced to choose sides. They both managed to protect us from that.

Lori never had a job when we were growing up, not even a part-time one. Even after Marie and I were in school for several years, she never once went out and found a job. We lived in Worcester, where there were jobs every ten feet. She had no fire, no passion and no drive. To me, this was the saddest part; the way she just wasted her life. I was a huge fan of TV news shows as a kid and I remember watching government officials talking one night about requiring anyone who collected from the state to do volunteer services. When I saw the story, I just laughed at the very idea of Lori volunteering. She would never do that. I never once saw her do something to help someone without looking for something in return. She was kind and nice to her friends, but if she gave them a joint she would want one back when they got their paycheck. The same went for a beer. If Lori bought the party bowl for you, you'd better believe she expected you to buy her one the next time you went out. There were always strings attached. She would never bake cookies for a bake sale or donate her time to clean up the broken glass and garbage around the projects. Lori volunteering? Now that would be funny!

Lori still struggles with her demons. She has done anything and everything possible to try to avoid or ignore them. As she gets older, it's clearly getting harder for her to tuck them away. She tried to kill herself last fall. This was a first as far as I know. I was driving into work as a Drug Abuse Resistance Education officer in my DARE van. I turned my work phone on because I was officially "on duty" and had to call into my dispatch. There was a voicemail on the screen. The message was from a nurse at the Athol Memorial Hospital. The woman said that my mother was there and that it was very important that I call right away. Before I dialed the phone, I thought for sure this was it. My heart started to race and I could feel a little panic set it. I always knew my mother would die young. She is in her late 50s but looks as if she is 70. Her skin is gray, and her eyes are yellow from a failing liver. Her Hepatitis C has been killing her because she has refused to take her medication. She won't take the pills because drinking alcohol would make her violently ill. This is an argument we have had too many times to count. Her doctor has been upfront and honest about the whole thing. Lori knows that the way she's living will kill her. Anyhow, I thought for sure they were going to tell me that she was dying or that she had overdosed.

When I got through, the very kind voice on the other end of the phone told me that Lori had cut her wrist and officers were called because she was screaming in her apartment. They found her alone, without any clothing on. She was having a breakdown because her most recent boyfriend had broken up with her. The end result was Lori being held against her will and transported to a hospital in western Massachusetts, where she was put on a locked-down floor for evaluations, a four-hour drive from my house; a seven-hour drive for Marie.

I spoke to my mother briefly. I did not tell her that the nurse had filled me in. She told me that she was having a hard time. She talked about the recent break-up. Lori said that she loved the man. They had been dating for a couple of months. I knew of the man. I knew that they had met at the bar and that he had given her a radio for her apartment. I did not know that the relationship had gone this far. According to Lori, the man had not talked to her in over a week. She said that she was lonely and didn't want to be alone. Lori admitted to cutting her wrists in an attempt to end her life. She assumed that a neighbor heard her screaming from her apartment and called the police. I told her that I was sorry that she was so sad. I told her I loved her and that Marie and I would probably be down within the next couple of days. She was grateful for my kind words. I could hear the relief in her voice. I asked if I could call Marie right away. She agreed that her children should know what had happened. We hung up and I called Marie to fill her in. Marie was instantly upset on the phone but not surprised. She went into responsible mode and asked what she could do. She was willing to drive down to Massachusetts right then. I told her I would find out what the doctors had to say and figure out when we could go visit. Marie and I had not been speaking much at this point. She had two children now and a new job. I was busy with my crazy life, and so we had drifted. This instantly brought us back together. We both knew our roles. We would do whatever it took to help Lori and to be there for one another.

Marie and I made plans to go and visit Lori as soon as they would allow visitors. When we got to the hospital she was in good spirits. She was very happy to see us and spoke like a child excited for a play date. We sat and talked for 45 minutes about nothing really important. I asked her if she liked the hospital food and if she was getting enough sleep. She didn't have any clothes with her and I told her I was willing to get her something at the closest shop. "No, I'm fine," she said. "They gave me some clothes from the lost and found. What I could really use are some cigarettes..." I refused to buy cigarettes so I didn't even acknowledge her request. She knew that I wouldn't. After we had been there awhile, Lori told us she really wanted a coffee. "That would be great," I said. "We can all go and have one together."

"No, you don't understand," Lori replied. "I want to have coffee alone and so I want you to leave now."

At this point I just looked at Marie, and we both stood up and left. Marie was speechless. She was silent for a while. I am sure she was processing what had just happened. We both agreed that the trip was a waist of time. I drove my four hours back home and then Marie continued her additional three hours and was home in time to have dinner with her family. This was the last time I saw Lori.

I have received a few calls from Lori since I visited her at the hospital that day. She was completely shit-faced each time. She has been excited to tell me about her new boyfriend and I remind her that she told me about him the last time that she called. I could hear him sitting in the background, making comments about whatever it was that he was watching on TV. He had no consideration for the fact that my mother was on the phone with her daughter. That was all I needed to know about him. I changed the topic quickly when she talked about her new love. She moved on and asked why I didn't send her a birthday card or any money. I could have replied with cutting words about how she hadn't sent any of us even a cheap card from the dollar store in years and so why did she have the nerve to ask why I didn't send her a card. I could have attacked her about how selfish she had been and how hurt Marie and I were when she dismissed us after only 45 minutes in the hospital. Instead, I made a choice: I hung up the phone. I need a break from Lori for a while.

4

Marie

My big sister Marie is the person that knows me best and still she has no idea about many of the terrible things I am going to share in this book. We have the same parents and so we have always had a strong bond. We lived together most of our young lives. We were the only true support for one another for most of our young adult lives.

Marie was born in Worcester but my parents moved with her to Jackson, Maine not long after she was born. My father and mother lived in a small cottage next to my grandparents' farmhouse. It was a tiny cottage but perfect for the new family. Our father and mother both worked in the chicken factory in Belfast. Belfast is a coastal community about a 30-minute drive from the farm. This was the closest area to the farm for any real employment opportunities. Our grandmother Doris took care of Marie while they were gone. There were many times that she would have to keep Marie overnight because our parents would come home late after stopping off for a few drinks after work, and were in no shape to care for an infant. Our parents were 20 years old when they had Marie. Clearly, they were not ready to be responsible parents. Doris has never touched a drop of alcohol or smoked a single cigarette her entire life. She had seen what they could do to a person growing up and always said she had no use for them. All of the grandkids, and there were seven at the time, used to pick on Marie, saying she was gram's favorite. That was ok with me because the relationship was special and I was happy Marie had that with someone. To this day they are still very close. Grandma Doris always looked after Marie and now Marie looks after her.

Grandma Doris was a mother to Marie and it is my opinion that it is because of their relationship that Marie managed to make it out of the projects and break the cycle.

When Lori was pregnant with me, the family fell apart. She moved Marie down to Massachusetts with her. I wish for Marie's sake that she had let her stay with Grandma Doris in Maine. Marie needed Doris. She was not cut out for the city. She is a soft soul and soft souls get crushed too easily in the projects. She deserved better. I don't know what her younger years looked like. I am not sure she remembers much. I do know that she spent a lot of time in the hospital due to an issue with her legs and her growth but I don't have any of those details. I was just told that one of her legs was longer than the other and so she needed surgery when she was very young.

Marie and I didn't look or act anything alike. She is a little taller than I am. She has brown hair and the same kind of big blue eyes my mother has. She refuses to color her hair wear makeup even though I've told her that a little mascara would make her eyes pop! But Marie doesn't care about that stuff. She is not out to impress anyone. She doesn't get caught up in anything superficial. Marie is and always has been the "real deal." She is definitely the most important family member that I have in my life, other than my children, of course. She is my voice of reason, the only person that can tell me to "shut up" in the most loving way and to "listen up", without me going off. I still have my Worcester spunk when I need it. Marie and I look after each other by being honest and upfront with one another. She also knows almost everything about me. She knows most of my secrets, and the good – and bad – choices that I've made over time. Whatever she didn't know before, she'll learn from reading my story here.

Marie is my big sister but most of the time I felt like the big sister. She was just more laid back than me. She definitely knows how to "go with the flow" better than I do. I have a hard time standing by and remaining quiet. She was wise beyond her years and I believe her survival was due to her ability to walk away and let go of things that she couldn't control. Marie never really complained. She just always made it known that she hated the city and wanted to live in Maine with Grandma Doris.

Marie was 11 years old when she moved to Maine. I was just nine and suddenly it was just Andrew, Jessie and I. At that point in time I knew this was the right choice for her. She was constantly being beat up and seen as an easy target. I couldn't always be around. We would practice fight in hopes of making her stronger but she just didn't have it in her. She was not a fighter. She never wanted to hurt anyone, even if they were pummeling her. She belonged in the country and I was not about to stand in her way.

When my father came down to get her, he was troubled. He sat at our kitchen table and told my mother that he didn't want to split us up. He knew how much we had depended on one another. My mother didn't have anything to say and so I stepped in. I told my father that I would be fine and that Marie needed to go. She was miserable here and the project kids wouldn't leave her alone. I could hold my own but I couldn't always be there and she had had her ass whooped more times than any person ever should for absolutely no reason, other than the fact that she was a skinny peanut and she would not fight back. My father listened to my argument and agreed to take her without me. I watched Marie as she collected a few final items. She was relieved. I could see it on her face and in her body language. She finally began to relax. Marie knew that she was going to be better off. I was not ready to leave, not yet. We promised to call each other every Sunday. Marie put her bags in that car and we were separated for about four years.

Marie has her own story. It is hers' to tell and perhaps one day she will do just that. What I can say is that today she is a loving wife and mother – she has found a way to move on from the dark days of her past.

5

Irish Twins

My brother Andrew was born when I was six years old. He was a fantastic distraction. Just less than twelve months later came Jessie, my youngest sister. They were Irish twins. Dave was absolutely thrilled about being a father. Lori knew what to expect. She seemed to roll with the new additions. Dave on the other hand walked around like the proudest father in the neighborhood. He did everything for the babies. He was up before the sun walking the floors. Watching his face as he held Andrew always made me smile. I would help him as much as I could.

Jessie was a beautiful baby! She looked like a porcelain doll. As she grew, it became clear that something was wrong with her. The drugs and the alcohol demons that my mother struggled with had a clear effect on Jessie. She was delayed in every aspect of her growth: she cried a lot as a baby and small child. She couldn't speak clearly. It wasn't until she was about six years old that it was discovered that she had been suffering from chronic ear infections. The crying was a result of the pain she was in. Her speech to this day is still affected. She has several learning disabilities and will never be able to live on her own without assistance.

I took care of Jessie and Andrew after Dave moved away. The relationship was on and off throughout the years. When Dave was not around I changed their diapers, fed them, and bathed them. I made sure that they were dressed in the morning. I mothered them. I remember potty-training Andrew. He was a quick study. He picked it up in a week or two. I didn't exactly know what I was doing but we figured it out together. He still jokes with me to this day about the way I taught him to wipe his front and back. Luckily, some friends at school filled in the blanks for him.

Jessie has struggled her entire life, and as we grew older we also grew farther apart. Jessie and I do not have a relationship anymore. I have tried on several occasions to include her in my life. Each time has ended in some kind of a fight and hurt feelings. The last occasion that I spent time with her I was terrified that I was going to lose my job and for me that was enough to cut ties. I thought that I had a fantastic idea for the two of us to spend some quality time together. I brought Jessie to Maine one week during the summer when I was living in York and just getting my feet wet at York PD. I planned a weekend trip to North Conway with a dear friend of her family and mine. I thought it would be a great idea to bring Jessie on a mini vacation. We rented a condo so that everyone would have plenty of space. I took Jessie shopping one of the days, visiting whatever outlets she wanted. I bought her bags of clothes. I knew that she did not have much and I was feeling very grateful for all that I had. I wanted to share a piece of my new life with her.

We spent time at the pool relaxing and had family-style dinners at night, but I could tell that Jessie was feeling "off" wherever we went. She seemed hostile or upset most of the time. I didn't understand why she was acting this way. I must have asked her a dozen times if she was ok. I was at a complete loss. I kept my attitude upbeat and hoped that she would get over whatever it was and embrace where she was and what she was doing. Unfortunately, this was too much for her to handle.

We left North Conway and headed back to York. Jessie was going to stay with me a few more days in my apartment before I took her home. On the ride home, Jessie was very angry. She was getting worse and I didn't know what had triggered this aggression. When I asked her what was wrong, she started screaming at me and punching me. I had to pull the car over. She continued her outburst by punching the dash of my car and calling me every four-letter name she could come up with. Thankfully, my police training kicked in and I remained calm and tried talking her down. At first, this didn't work so I had to wait for her to run out of energy. To be completely exhausted.

When she finally stopped I asked her to please just sit there so that we could make it home. At this point I wasn't comfortable putting her in the back seat. I could imagine her grabbing me from behind while I was driving. The remainder of the ride home was quiet. We didn't speak. When we returned to York I told Jessie that we would talk about it in the morning. I went to bed but I was not able to sleep. To be honest, I didn't know what she was capable of anymore. I did not trust her enough to even allow myself to sleep. She was not the little pig-tailed blonde I had helped to raise. Her demons were dark and the poor thing had no idea how to control them. That kind of rage can never be trusted or taken for granted.

When morning came, I took care of breakfast and then sat next to Jessie and asked her what had happened. She instantly became angry again. Her features changed and she looked like a different person, the same fiercely out-of-control person she had become when she was hitting me in my car. She was not my sister. I don't know who she was but she most definitely was not my sister. She told me that I thought I was better than her and that I was nothing but a piece of shit. I couldn't understand where this was coming from. I had done everything in my power to give her a special weekend. Jessie was filled with rage. I didn't deserve it but she had nowhere else to put it. She stood up screaming and swearing at me. She grabbed my coffee table and threw it across the room. I grabbed her by the arms and threw her to the floor. I held her down until she stopped. She hated me right then and she wanted to hurt me. Jessie was bigger than I was at this time. She punched and clawed me until I got hold of her arms and pinned her down.

I kept repeating, "stop this" and "calm down" until she eventually she did. I was bawling my eyes out at this point. I was so hurt and confused. I went into police mode and used my training to control her until she was exhausted and finally stopped.

I called the on-duty sergeant for two reasons. The first was to make sure no one had called the police concerned about the yelling and fighting. The second was to let him know that I would not be in for work that night. I would be driving my sister home. She was going back to Massachusetts. I couldn't handle her and I knew she needed more help than I could offer. I called her father Dave and let him know we were on our way. Jessie sat in the back seat this time and didn't speak a word. When we got to her house, Andrew met me with a big hug and told me how sorry he was. Dave wanted to know what had happened and if I had done something to provoke her. I was offended at first but realized quickly that he was just very protective of his little girl that was not so little anymore.

Jessie went to her room and went through the bags of clothes I had bought her. She was so proud and smiling as she showed her father the stuff I had bought her. It was as if nothing had happened. I sat with Dave before I left, over a cup of coffee. This is when he informed me that she had been going through a lot of medical testing and that the belief was that she, like Lori, was bipolar. After being diagnosed, Jessie was put on medication but whether she's taking her pills is another story. Jessie has been abusing drugs on and off for the past several years. She has been living in group homes and women's shelters as well as hotels with different boyfriends. She had a couple girlfriends along the way as well. I am sad for Jessie because she never had a real chance. Her head is so messed up and she just didn't get the support she so desperately needed. I still love her dearly but I cannot bring her into my children's life. I could never forgive myself if something happened and frankly they do not need to be exposed to that kind of frightening and dangerous behavior. I will do whatever it takes to keep them young as long as possible.

Now Andrew is another story. He was a busy little man forced to grow up way too fast. When he was a child, he had light brown hair and big blue eyes that sparkled when he smiled. As long as I can remember he had an adorable bowl cut. He was a free spirit for sure. My little buddy. He came to me with any questions or worries he would have.

I tucked him into bed every night and got him dressed for school every day until he could do it on his own. He was a quick study. He tried very hard to please me. Though we were only six years apart in age, I felt as if I mothered him. It was never a burden. One smile from Andrew and you were forced to smile too. You could lose your fingers in his dimples and his laugh was contagious.

He was running around the projects with friends at age five unsupervised. He would stay close by but went in and out of the house as he pleased. Lori did have enough sense to bring him in at night. I would leave with friends and when I returned he was the first check in. He would get so excited to see me. He was usually filthy, covered in the dirt of the projects, and you could scrape it off of the bottom of his feet with your fingernail. Lori would ask me to give him a bath because he wouldn't do it for her. Again, I didn't mind. He was my little buddy.

Andrew would occasionally get into mischief. One summer day he must have been bored because he took a black sharpie and marked up one of the cars in the lot. We never had a car. Dave had his license but I don't remember him having a car once we got to the projects. We never went anywhere and if we did, we took the bus. The owner of the car that Andrew had defaced was a very large Hispanic woman, and when she came to confront my mother, she was boiling with anger. It did not go well. "I'm going to make you pay for the paint job!" the woman shouted to Lori. "And you'd better get your head out of your ass and pay attention to your kids before they do any more damage!"

Lori didn't say anything. She just sat on the cement steps and waited for the rant to be over. My mother's silence only fueled the woman's anger even more: she grabbed onto Lori's long brown hair and threw her down to the ground. She then slapped Lori in the face several times until my mother pled for her to stop. This was not something I expected. Lori was a fighter. She didn't take shit from anyone. She had once sliced a grown man with a knife without hesitation. What was different this time?

I remember screaming at my mother, "Fight back! Fight back!" This got the woman's attention, and when she turned to look at me, I was standing off to the side, crying hysterically. She stopped hitting my mother and walked back home but not before making it very clear that she would be expecting her money at the first of the month. Lori stood up and brushed herself off without saying a word. She seemed fine, as if now that she had taken her beating, the situation was over and done and she was ready to move on. But the thing that really stayed with me from this incident was how none of the adults who had stood by and watched this fight had uttered a single word. No one said anything to intervene. No one called the police. It was clear that you handled your own shit and then moved on. We were all in the same boat and there was, as there often is, an *us versus them* attitude when it came to the police. I was just happy to be on the side of my family that day. That was not the time to show my allegiance to the force. I would have had my ass handed to me for sure. But after that happened, I knew in my heart that law enforcement was going to be my path. I was going to be on the side of justice. I just didn't know how it was going to happen.

Lori would never be considered a saver. We had no nest egg. We all knew that after Andrew's little adventure, the next state check would be a little lighter since she would be paying for the paint job. The funny thing was, my mother never hit Andrew. She was definitely comfortable with swatting our behinds with a belt (or anything else) on a regular basis to keep us in line, but this time she did nothing. I think she felt bad that we had all seen that fight. She knew she should have been watching him more closely instead of letting him run around the cars in the parking lot. Andrew had to stay inside for two days but then Lori let him return to his regular play. He felt awful about what had happened. He learned his lesson very quickly. I don't think he touched a marker again for a very long time. Lori fell back into her regular routine thus allowing Andrew to be out and about on his own yet again. Andrew was a smart kid. I had no doubt he would figure out how to play the game and survive the projects quickly. This was his first major lesson.

6

The COPS are coming

I knew that I wanted to be a police officer as far back as I could remember. I would cringe in my bed, listening to all those late-night parties, which usually ended in knock-down fights, and that solidified my drive. Fight after fight. Night after night. I was always feeling scared or worried, and kept begging for them to stop. The yelling would cut through me, and I'd tremble with anxiety and fear at what I heard: the violent anger of one human being beating the piss out of the other. There was no way to shut out the knowledge that someone I loved was either on the giving or receiving end of that pain.

I called the police more times than I can remember. The cops in Worcester rode two in a car, just like in all the TV shows I watched. They had dark blue uniforms and there was usually at least one very tall officer in the pair. I loved the sight of their badges: they were shiny and covered their hearts. I always thought that was special. I wanted a badge that would protect my heart, too.

I also loved the way the cops seemed to be fearless as they came in and took care of business. Sometimes, the person they were taking would go willingly but other times they'd get somebody who would put up a fight. I watched them drag man after man out of our apartment. I remember one who had his ass hanging out of his pants. He thrashed back and forth and even spit at the officers. This didn't stop them. As far I could tell, they always won. This was a time before Tasers or even pepper spray. They

53

used sticks and handcuffs, but I never saw them pull a gun. I don't think I could have handled that back then.

When the cops came to my house I was happy because they always made the fighting stop. Sometimes they took in my mother or whatever man she was with. Other times the police would separate the two for the night so that we could all go to bed. Watching my mother placed into handcuffs was never easy. I was conflicted. I wanted the fighting to stop. I wanted her to learn her lesson. I wanted her to get help. I knew we would be fine while she was gone and I knew she would be home the next day. I was never afraid of the police. I understand why children become afraid or angry when officers take their parents away. For me, I was relieved. I needed a break. I needed a good nights sleep without the anxiety that came with listening to the fighting. It wasn't always Dave Whenever he and Lori would break up; there would be the occasional fill-in boyfriend who would typically last for a month or two. Usually until he beat my mother so bad that he went to jail and my mother would draw the line in the sand. A few weeks later Dave would be back and things would return to normal – at least for a while. I really do believe they loved each other. They lived well together when they were sober but when they started using again, their insecurities would creep out, leading to a blow-up of emotions and violence. My mother was famous for breaking furniture. After she was diagnosed as being bipolar, her extreme actions began to make more sense to me.

My drive to go into law enforcement grew stronger and stronger with every bad experience I had. One would think it would be the other way around; that I would start to hate the people that put my family in jail. Instead, I loved them. They always made the fighting stop and helped to ease my fear. The police were my superheroes and I wanted to be a superhero someday, too.

I didn't reveal this secret dream to anyone until I was finishing high school. I never felt comfortable telling people what I was going to do with my life. The people in my life didn't like the police. My family feared getting caught doing whatever it was that they were doing. My friends in the Valley hated any kind of authority figure because we wanted to do what we wanted to do. For me, it wasn't about ordering people around or taking them to jail. It was about taking fear away. It was about being a kind voice in a very dark place. It was about wiping the tears away. The thought of a child being afraid or hurt maddens me. I become a different person. Now, as a Drug Abuse Resistance Education (DARE) officer, I am very assertive with the adults but still mothering to any child I come in contact with. That's the reason I was put on this earth: to help our kids. I went through what I went through for that experience and knowledge I gained. My life has been a gift and I will continue to pass it along.

I saw another side of the officers on a summer day when we, the project kids, were all in the playground basketball courts watching some of the bigger kids battle it out in a game of basketball. Just a couple of weeks before, a guy from the neighborhood was shot at night on that same court. But we weren't thinking about that as we stood around in the sunshine watching the game. I was with two of my friends as a police car pulled up and two officers got out of the car. You could hear their radios squawking. They were both smiling. I remember thinking *Oh, shit, who are they going to take in today?*

To all of our surprise, one of the young officers asked if he could play ball. I remember my body filling with joy and I had a huge smile on my face. What a great thing to do! These cops didn't have to do this. They could have driven by like everyone else with their windows up and air conditioning going. They could have acted like they didn't see us. The crowd went wild with cheers and the games began. The cops got smoked, of course. Our guys played ball all of the time. That's all that they had to do. It was a blast to watch. There were slam dunks, shouts of "Take that!" and lots of cheers. These unexpected visitors made the day special for all of us! Before the officers left they came over and gave us high fives. They asked us our names and thanked us for letting them come into our yard. One of the officers offered each of us a piece of Trident gum. It was amazing! I never had the luxury of gum and the fact that a police officer gave it to me made it taste even better.

I remember promising myself that I was going to do that one day. I was going to pull up in my police car, give the kids with blank looks on their faces a big smile, and challenge them to a little game. I have kept that promise more times than I can count and every time I do I think back to that summer day on the courts in the Valley.

My partners think I am silly when I grab the mic in the cruiser leading off a parade. I yell to the kids and get them excited. I tell them to cheer and shout that I want to see them smile. When I use my little kid voice, they go crazy! My first year as the DARE officer I took it upon myself to get into the middle of the gym floor during the Halloween dance and do the chicken dance. I did this for two reasons. The first is, it was a blast – especially with my daughter right beside me. The second was that the kids got to see me as a silly person and not as someone that would take them away to jail if they did something wrong. That is the last thing that I ever want a child to think and that is the worst thing that a parent could ever tell their child. Children should *trust* the police. We are the people that devote our lives to keeping them safe. When young people are taught to fear the police, it is a true disservice to them. They will have no one to turn to if a family member hurts them or if they are in over their heads. Unfortunately, we do live in a world where people that we love, the ones we are closest to, harm us. This is why I go into those classrooms and sit on the floor with the kiddos. This is why I offer high fives and hugs to my "little people," as I call them. Not every cop has a soft spot for kids but every police officer takes a vow to serve and protect, and society needs to give them the opportunity to do just that.

7

Survival of the Fittest

As I have said before, I figured out how to survive at a very young age. Basic needs were a challenge for my family. Everything that we had was handed down from someone and we were barely able to hold it together. Some things I just couldn't go without and so I learned how to steal without getting caught. I mastered it by the time I was eight or nine years old. Looking back, I still can't believe the nerve that I had as a young girl. For example, Shoes were not easy to come by. Every few months I would need to get a new pair. I remember walking to school in broken down shoes. I could feel the cold pavement on my feet. I didn't bother asking my mother because I knew what the answer was going to be. I had to figure out a way to get a pair of shoes on my own and figure it out I did.

The first time I stole shoes I was between four and five. It was before we moved to the Valley. I used to walk to the city pool with a bunch of kids. I was the youngest one of the group and it was a long walk and my feet were sore. My shoes were all worn out. I needed new shoes and just couldn't put if off any longer. Walking up a set of cement stairs to the pool area, I saw a pair of Cabbage Patch shoes that looked like they were my size. It was as if someone had placed them there just for me. I was so excited. All I could think about was how badly I needed new shoes and then -- just like that! -- they were there. I looked around, wondering who they belonged to. I couldn't tell because there were so many people at the pool. There was a towel and a couple of bracelets next to the shoes. I didn't care about them. I didn't need a towel; I could air dry. I didn't need the bracelets; they were not going to help my aching feet. Also, I thought for sure the owner would be mad if the bracelets were gone. But I did need those shoes. My friends and I went about our business, splashing and playing in the pool. Afterwards, we lay down on the cement, to catch some rays. I couldn't get the thought of those shoes out of my head. I watched to see if anyone showed interest in them. But no one went back to get them. I told myself that the girl who owned them probably had three pairs at home. I justified stealing the shoes to myself. I told myself that I needed them and she did not. I convinced myself that her parents would just go out and buy her another pair tomorrow. I was comfortable with my decision at this point. If those shoes were still there when it was time to leave, then they were going home with me. I had a long walk home and I needed them!

Marie was in charge of me on this adventure. She let me know it was time to go. I walked over to the green-and-white Cabbage Patch kids' shoes, and looked around. I was a little anxious but I had a plan if the owner suddenly came running up. I would explain that I thought the shoes were mine. "After all," I'd say, very innocently, "I would never intentionally steal something that belonged to somebody else." I slipped my shoes off so that she would at least have those to get home, and I put on my new shoes. They felt so good! Just like a brand-new pair. I felt instant relief pressing my toes down into the padding of the shoes. I was smiling from head to toe.

Marie never even noticed my new shoes. No one did. If they did, they didn't say a word. It's funny to think about now. How could they *not* notice? For me, the walk home was wonderful. I had a new bounce in my step and a huge smile on my face. La di da!!!! When I got home I told my mother that I had found the shoes next to a tree. She had no reaction. She didn't care where or how I had gotten the shoes. This started a trend that lasted several years. If I needed shoes, I'd always find a way to get them. I progressed from shoes to socks and packages of underwear. Finally, I moved on to clothes. It didn't take me long to figure this system out. Need versus want. I only took what I needed and not things that I wanted. I was proud of my self-control.

Zaire's, which soon turned into Ames, was in the Lincoln Street Plaza in Worcester. This was a small shopping center, with a drugstore, a Papa Gino's and a Big Boy's burger joint. It was about a 20-minute walk from the projects to the plaza. I made this trip at least once a week. Most of the time I was on my own. If I brought a friend, that was okay, too. I don't recall ever feeling scared for my safety. On one occasion, a male pulled up beside me and waved me over to his car to look in the window. He was about 30 years old and overweight. I knew enough to go to the passenger's side of the car. When I walked up I could see that he was masturbating. This shocked me for about a second and then I got mad and called the man a "fucking pig". He drove off as I screamed at him. I used my "big girl" voice. That voice we all have that demands attention and respect. That voice that makes it very clear you mean business. I startled him more than he had startled me. I don't know what came over me. I was just so pissed off that he would do this. After he drove away, I just kept walking. This was another occasion I never bothered to tell Lori about. She wouldn't care. I was proud of myself for not letting the disgusting man get the best of me. All I could think about was what of a piece of shit he was. At this time in my life I knew a lot of people that I thought of in this category. That is probably why I was not surprised. I still managed to get my shopping in that day. I was not going to let him ruin it.

Zaire's was my favorite place to hit up. People never questioned me. They never stopped me. The employees always smiled at me. I have no doubt that this was because I was a little blonde-haired girl with a big smile. I never looked or felt nervous. I convinced myself that I could talk myself into doing anything. I saw the way clerks at the store watched the other kids from the projects. The kids with the darker skin. They didn't think I was one of them. I was clearly from the other side of town. I knew I had them fooled. I breezed in with my head held high, and walked around the store, checking things out. I would work my way over to the shoes. I didn't mess around. I kicked my worn out, sole less shoes under a display and put on a pair of new shiny white shoes. I'd think to myself, *I will be good for a while now.* I didn't go for the expensive shoes or the character shoes. I didn't need those. I didn't go for heels even though I desperately wanted "girly" shoes. I didn't want to bring attention to myself. At a very young age, I knew to just take what I needed and move on. It was how I survived. I wasn't a thief; I was a kid that needed a pair of shoes. To this day if I have a student that needs a pair of shoes I make sure that they have them by the end of the week. I guess this is my way of paying the shoes back.

Clothing was a different story. Most of the clothes that I owned I would take from the lost and found piles at school. It was too risky to steal clothes from a store. They were larger and harder to cover up. I could shove socks up the arm of my sleeve or underwear down my pants but sweatshirts and pants were too risky. This girl was no fool! The best thing I took was when I was walking through the projects and I was feeling really cold. It was late fall and I only had a short-sleeve T-shirt on. I was shivering and had goose bumps all over. I looked over at the clotheslines and saw a green large sweatshirt that said, "Don't Worry Be Happy" in yellow lettering. I laughed out loud because I knew that was the perfect sweatshirt for me. I walked over without hesitation and took the shirt off the line. I pulled it right on and walked away. I was smiling from ear to ear. I was no longer cold and frankly I loved the sweatshirt. It was about three sizes too large for me but that made it even better. I never took more than I needed and if I could get what I needed from the lost and found I was more than happy with that. I stole the shoes from the store because that was the only place to get them -- besides the pool, that is.

There is another form of survival that was crucial to my childhood -- fighting. Before moving to the Valley, we lived in the factory part of Worcester on Tanner Street. Marie and I would walk back and forth to school, sometimes just the two of us and other times with kids from the neighborhood. It seemed like every other day someone would want to pick a fight with one of us. Even though I was younger, Marie was usually the target. Her nickname was "Bones" because she was so skinny. She was also very quiet and wouldn't speak up for herself.

I learned very quickly that I would need to learn how to fight and by fight I mean kick ass. I also knew how to run my mouth in a way that made kids even bigger than me think twice. I was a little shit. I can admit that now. I had a big mouth and an attitude to go right along with it. I know I was no older than six because that's when we moved to the Valley. I started school early. Massachusetts didn't have the October birthday rule then. Anyhow, I would ask the neighborhood boys to fight with me. I would ask each of them to punch me and in return I would get a chance to punch them back. We wrestled on the ground, going at each other with all our strength. I did whatever I could to become stronger. I needed to be able to fight back. I knew I couldn't beat everyone, but at least they were going to know that I had been there, and dammit they did! Nothing was off limits! On Tanner Street or the Valley. I would fight boys and girls. I would fight two girls at the same time until they ran off crying to their mothers. I would punch, claw, rip out hair, and even bite if I had to. Let me be clear: I never started a fight but I was never going to run away from one either. If I lost the fight, which was rare, I would never let them see me cry. I was too proud for that. I didn't care how bad it hurt, I would not let myself cry. As soon as I got away from the crowd, I would let go and that's when my tears would come. After I was done crying, I would break down where I had gone wrong and create a plan for the next time I was in that situation. I would work harder and get stronger. I would learn from my mistakes. If they found a weakness, I would make sure to correct it for the future. I was tactical in my thinking even back then, like I was playing a chess match. I was a survivor.

I took on the responsibility of protecting Marie. She was kind, sweet, and loving with a natural, mothering demeanor. I am sure she wiped my rear more than once when I was in diapers and I vaguely remember the baths we would take together when she was in charge of washing us both. I used to love the way she would French braid my hair. Marie was a good older sister but it was no secret that she couldn't stand up for herself. She didn't have the fire I had.

Learning how to fight was something I had to do for her and for myself. I knew even in kindergarten that I would need to be able to fight. Thinking about that makes me so sad. I never had a chance to be a child. I had to worry about food, clothing, fighting off so many people. I had to *survive*! This is probably why I am such a goober now! I love to play and I mean play! I will sled all day with my kiddos or color in a *My Little Pony* coloring book for as long as I possibly can. I love being outside, and can disappear for hours in the woods, running or hiking trails. This is when I am my happiest. I have been very fortunate to be able to make up for the lost time that I had growing up. I plan on doing this for the rest of my life!

When it came time for my background check at York Police Department I lost a couple of nights' sleep worrying about how I was going to tell them about this part of my past. I didn't know if my soon-to-be bosses would understand why I did what I did. I wondered if they would look at me differently and judge me. I don't regret my choices. I did what I had to do to survive. I had to provide for myself, even when I was as young as four and five years old. I am amazed that I knew as much as I did when I did! I am also extremely grateful for that fighter's mentality. I would not have survived without it. Thankfully, my bosses understood and a couple of them said it helped them to relate to me better. We all have our stories that are part of our past. I wouldn't change mine for anything. I hope that it makes me a better officer and friend for my students.

8

Lincoln Street Elementary School

Lincoln Street School was just over a mile from Great Brook Valley. It was an old brick building that housed kindergarten to sixth grade students. The kids from the projects as well as from more middle-class families came together at the school for their free education. The building was overflowing with students. There were trailers in the back of the building to help accommodate the overflow of students. The cafeteria was on the basement floor. The playground was small and simple. We had a few swings and basketball hoops. Most of my classmates had no idea I came from the projects and I didn't tell them otherwise. The white kids had houses and the Hispanic and black kids lived in the projects. This wasn't something we really talked about until I was about 11 years old. Elementary kids are naturally kind and accepting, and I never felt different from the other white kids. I am sure that they knew I was poor but they never made me feel poor. We were all friends and treated each other equally. I never felt insecure at Lincoln Street School. I never had a reason to. I kept my home problems to myself and my time at school was just that, my time.

When I was around nine or ten years old I was told by my teachers at the Lincoln Street School that I had dyslexia. Frankly, I was surprised that was all that I had. I was pulled out of my classes in the fourth grade and given tests to determine if I had any learning disabilities. I sat with a man with a stop clock and he timed how fast I could figure problems out. On another occasion, I had to read out loud, which was one of my least favorite things to do at the time, and then explain what I had just read. Dyslexia held me back but it didn't hold me down. Despite getting help from in-school tutors and ed techs in the resource room, I struggled with reading and reading comprehension for most of my school years. However, I thrived in math and social studies. I was good with numbers and had no problem memorizing equations and formulas. As for social studies, I loved history and still do. I was interested in how we came to be where we are and who made changes happen in our country. I realized early on that I needed to find reading material that sparked that interest. If I did, my passion for a subject could help me read anything -- even if I had to read it three times in order to get it. If I didn't connect with the material, I barely treaded water. I did enough to pass but I never tapped into my full potential. I passed on to the next grade and I always knew enough to be respectful to my teachers. I saw that the kids who struggled with basic social skills, such as showing respect, struggled their entire lives. I knew enough *not* to be one of those kids.

At school, they told us to "Say no to drugs" and I absolutely knew that was the right thing to do. When I was home, I would pick out the seeds and help my mother roll her joints, again, because I knew that was the right thing to do. It was as if I lived two separate lives. When I went to Lincoln Street School, I was a little girl who said "please" and "thank you" -- to the point of it being obnoxious. I didn't want anyone to think that I was not respectful at school. In the Valley, I was seen as a spunky little, loud-mouthed kid that could chew you up one side and down the other. Kids didn't know what hit them when I went on the attack. I could smack down anyone, crush any comeback, and swear like a trucker. It is amazing how quickly I could adjust to my surroundings.

These two worlds clashed when I was in the second grade. My science project was on drugs. (After all, I figured I knew all there was to know about drugs: what they looked like, smelled like, and even tasted like.) The base of my project was a Budweiser case box that I took from our cupboard. I put things that looked like different drugs that I was familiar with into baggies and taped them to the box. Lori was interested in what I was doing. When I told her about my project she just smiled and said, "Well, that's an idea" and continued whatever it was that she was doing. She was never interested in my schoolwork. We never did homework together or sat down and read a book. The responsibility of my education fell completely on my teachers and me. Lori did not have a role.

On the day of the science fair I was both nervous and excited! I couldn't wait to present my project. The judges were all white older men and women who wore nice clothes and seemed to take their role as judges very seriously. They walked up and down the aisles of tables interviewing the students. I usually had a knack for talking to people, but this time I was afraid of what the judges were going to think of my cardboard project made from scraps that I dug up from around our apartment.

When the two judges came around to look at my project they seemed very impressed. One of the judges asked, "How does a little girl in the second grade know so much about drugs?"

I needed to think quickly. Since DARE was a big deal back then, I responded with, "I learned a lot from DARE. I also learned a lot from my mother."

I don't think they really understood what I meant. Anyhow, they bought my explanation and moved on, after patting me on the head and telling me what a good job I had done.

At the end of the day my teacher pulled me aside and said that he had some news about the science fair. I wish I could remember his name. He was very kind and he was a great teacher. He treated all of his students as equals. I remember his hand on my shoulder and a sincere look on his face. He felt sad for me. He knew what he was about to tell me would hurt me. He said that there was a tie for first place in our grade. Cynthia, who did her project on the wheel and its inventor and me, the girl with the cardboard Budweiser box. He followed this by letting me know that the other teachers took a vote and since it was more likely that Cynthia would be able to attend the finals she would be taking the first place title.

The entire staff knew who I was and who my mother was. They also knew that she had never attended a single school event or meeting. She didn't come to the field day where I won three blue ribbons. She didn't come to the Christmas concert where I stood in the front row and sang my heart out. She didn't come to the parent-teacher workshops or informational nights. She would not bring me to the science fair. My consolation came from being in front of the class and having the teacher congratulate me. I know that he felt bad for me. I was a little sad as well but I knew that they were right. Cynthia was a better shot for our school to win.

After that year I really didn't try as hard on my projects. I did enough to get by. I always cared about my grades but as for the rest of it I would just tell myself "screw them" and move forward. If I acted like I didn't care, eventually I wouldn't. I thank God every day that this did not work for me. I could never just roll over and give up. Instead, I learned how to focus on the things that would make a real difference.

When I think about my days at Lincoln Street School, I don't think about how well I did in my classes. I think about the friends that I made. I think about how well I did fitting in. I never felt poor. I was never treated like I was poor. There was prejudice all around me. I was able to avoid this somehow. The wealthier kids, for the most part, didn't know I lived in the projects. If they did they didn't let me know. The project kids knew me as one of their own. I had only one obsession and that was for food. I was always hungry and by 10:00 a.m. on a typical school day, I was absolutely starving! I looked forward to school lunches every day. I absolutely loved having a hot lunch, Especially Tater Tots, green beans, and Salisbury steak with gravy. Thinking about it makes me smile. You couldn't pay me enough to eat a Salisbury steak now. Mac and Cheese was another favorite. Lunch at school was my only opportunity to have real milk and fresh fruit.

The lunch ladies were the best! They would make sure I had plenty of food on my tray. They knew I was on the free lunch list. I imagine they knew more than I thought they did at the time. They must have noticed that I would occasionally wear the same clothes for two to three days in a row. Most times, I would mix and match my outfits, trying to change it up so that they couldn't tell that the pants I was wearing were the same that I had worn all week. No one ever said anything to me about my clothes. I am really glad that they didn't! I would have added it to my list of worries.

I had a hard enough time getting out the door in the morning after making sure the kids were all set, and scrounging up whatever I could find to eat. Most mornings it was nothing and so I was grateful to have lunch around 11:00 a.m. I would gulp water at the fountain to help make it through. Thankfully, my friends and teachers were kind. If one of them had an extra granola bar or snack they would offer it to me. Acting as if they accidently packed two. I can remember as far back as in the first grade teacher. She always had something small for me. We would make deals. If I wore my glasses everyday I would get a prize on Fridays. It was usually a plastic bracelet or charm. She always had an apple just in case I wanted one. I always knew it was for me. She would look at the apple and then look at me with a smile. When there was a break I would walk up and grab it. I am sure the other kids noticed but they were *kind* enough not to say anything. It is no surprise that today I have a sign in my office titled Kindness. I make sure that my students read it when they come in to visit with me. I ask them if they understand what that means. Most times they hit it right on the head. They tell me how it is important to put others needs in front of our own. It is important to be nice to one another and to never intentionally try to hurt another person. I am impressed with the amount of compassion my little people have. I know to never take that for granted. That is a gift for all of us!

School buses were not an option for the project's kids. We walked to and from school every day, rain or shine. A black man by the name of JoJo would walk down the street blowing a whistle to let us all know to come out. His job was to make sure all of the project kids made it to school safely. We would run out to meet him on the sidewalk. I was one of a handful of white kids still living in this projects complex but I really didn't even realize it until I was a little older. These were my people and the kindness and friendships were stronger than anything I have ever known. We were all just trying to survive, despite rampant drug use, violence, and poverty. It was our way of life and we didn't know any different. JoJo was a fan of black soul music as well as a little Michael Jackson, and he would sing James Brown songs as we walked behind him. He was the type of adult that a child would gravitate to. He took his job very seriously, and never took a day off. If there was school, JoJo was there. We were safe with him. There was pride and purpose for JoJo looking after us. He lived in the projects with his wife and three children, about a mile up from where I lived.

JoJo was a jack of many trades. He had a soft heart for kids and did whatever he could to make a difference. JoJo and his wife offered an escape for the project kids after school and on weekends. They had a group of about 15 kids that would dance in a group called the P.Y.T.'s, Pretty Young Things, named after the song I'm sure. The group consisted of every make and model. The only requirements were that you lived in the projects, had a good attitude, and were under the age of 16.

I was a member of the P.Y.T.'s for about three years. Each of us paid 25 cents a week to dance in the group. The quarters went into a cloth bag that JoJo hid under a shelf in his living room. The money went towards our bus fare when we had "shows." We had about eight different routines. Organized with big kids in the back and little ones in the front. I don't know how he did it, but JoJo booked our shows at nursing homes throughout Worcester. It really was a fantastic plan to keep us out of trouble. There were more girls than boys in the group, and we'd have practice shows in different sections of the projects. We were good! We had moves and lots of rhythm.

I remember one occasion when we were going to have a practice show one block from our building. I told Lori, hoping she would check it out. She sat on the steps, drinking a beer, but she didn't come over to watch the show. There were people all around. The music was playing while people were clapping and cheering. Still, she just sat on her steps. I never asked why she didn't come over. But I didn't make an excuse for her either. I knew that it was complete bullshit that she had not made an effort to walk the one block and at least clap for me for five minutes. The show lasted just over an hour, and it was absolutely adorable -- and dammit I rocked my moves. I was mad at her for a few days, but I never told her that. It wouldn't have done any good. I made a promise to myself that I would always show up to support my children.

The P.Y.T's kept me out of trouble, and taught me that if you work hard and practice your passion you can do amazing things. I was a pop dancer. People clapped and cheered for me. I was in love with music. To this day, if a song comes on that reminds me of the P.Y.T's I can't help but bust a move. My kids get a kick out of it. JoJo was a gift to so many of the project kids. I know that he has since passed. My cousin Jason let me know when that happened. I am sure it was a packed service. He touched many lives and he kept a lot of us out of trouble, especially the girls. He knew exactly what he was keeping us away from, even if we didn't know it at the time.

9

Pay Day (a.k.a. "State Check Day")

The first of the month was always the most stressful time for our family. I was never

relieved that my mother would get her state check. Instead, I was anxious about who

was going to be at our place that night. Once it started to get late and the house was

filling up, Lori would put us in one bedroom and we would try to sleep with the loud

music and yelling. It was never a surprise when the cops came to tell them to quiet

down or to break up a fight. I have no idea where most of these people came from. It

was as if they knew the checks were coming in and wandered through the projects

looking for a party. A few of the people were neighbors but there was always a variety

of men and women I had never met or had seen only once or twice before -- always at

these parties. This made no sense to me. My mother had to have known that she was

being used, but she didn't care. She was up for a "good time" and as long as there

were people around, she was happy.

As I grew older, I became less reluctant to call the cops. I had had enough and I took

on that responsibility. I had to keep the others safe and I had to get some sleep. I

would sneak over to a neighbor's apartment or walk out and grab the phone when Lori

wasn't looking. I had this part down. The dispatcher was always nice to me. I am sure

she could tell I was young. I would either tell her that people were being too loud or that

someone was fighting. It all depended on the circumstances. I would never think to lie

to them. There was no point in it. I knew they were going to come, so why not just tell

them the truth? Lori never scolded me for calling them. I could tell by the look on her face that she knew I had called. When they did arrive, I think she was relieved in a way. Her life was so out of control and this forced her to keep herself in check for a short while, at least until the next payment came in.

I remember one night I heard yelling and a piece of furniture being thrown. I was in the room with the kids and Marie. I told them all to stay put. I just knew that this was a bad situation, and something in my stomach told me to be careful. Jessie was the newest addition to our family. She was just a baby. I remember her crying and how Marie and I tried to comfort her. I left the room slowly, creeping out of the door, and I saw that there was someone in the bathroom. As I got closer, I saw it was Dave. He was bleeding badly. There was blood all over the sink and bathroom floor, a trail that started in the living room and ended in the bathroom. He had a large gash on his forearm. Lori had grabbed a knife and cut him during their fight. They got into fights often, especially when the check would arrive and they had money for more than just beer. But it had never come to this before. Sure, there was always hitting and throwing furniture but never a knife. Dave was scared. I was scared for him! He looked at me and said, "She's fucking CRAZY!" I'll never forget the look on his face. This time she had gone too far.

I called the cops that night. I just told them to come. I didn't tell them about the knife. I knew that this was a game changer. I didn't lie but I didn't tell them the full story either. My mother stood speechless in the living room. The knife had been put away. I am not sure who hid the knife. It had seemed to just disappear. When the police came I did not say a word. Lori was scared. She just stared at me. Dave handled the cops. He told them it was an accident that he had cut himself. I know he was thinking about us. Dave is Andrew and Jessie's father but he was also like a father to me. His relationship with my mother was on and off for over 10 years. After the EMT's took Dave to the hospital for stitches, Lori passed out on the couch and I cleaned up the mess. I don't know what time Dave got home that morning. I just noticed my mother went out of her way to be nice to him for a while. We never discussed what happened that night. Dave carries that memory on his forearm still today. When I look at it, he just laughs and repeats how "crazy" my mother was. He doesn't get any argument from me.

After the knife incident they just took a couple weeks off to calm things down. It wasn't long before we were right back at it. This roller coaster never stopped -- it just slowed every down once in a while.

When the police come to your house in the projects, everyone knows about it. The blue lights bring out people the way the darkness brings out the roaches. Everyone around us knew what had happened. They also knew not to speak a word of the truth to the police. If they did, they would be looking for a new place to live very quickly. You were a member of a family. The family handles their shit amongst themselves. Dave has been sober for over 20 years now. He had that clarifying moment when he decided he wanted to be better. He wanted to live better for his children. He started with AA and still goes to this day. The relationship couldn't last between him and Lori. She refused to get sober. She tried a few times but could never make it. They live just a few miles away from each other now in a small town called Athol but they never see one another. Sadly, I don't see him often. When I do, I'm reminded how grateful I am that he did his best to keep my mother in check. Though it was an impossible task, he fought the battle for many years. He also made sure we had food in our bellies before we went to bed. Even if it was just white rice with butter or Ramen, he always made sure that we ate something. When Dave wasn't there, things were a lot more dicey. Unfortunately, most times we were on our own.

10

Food: Hungering for What We Didn't Have

You begin to realize how precious food truly is when you don't have any. We survived only because of food stamps, food pantries, and the hot lunch program. The feeling of hunger was something we felt just about every day. We were so used to it that it didn't really faze us. We would have to figure something out. It was often up to us to find food. As for nutrition, we didn't care about that. We just wanted to stop the ache. The food stamps would come in about the same time as the state check. We all knew when they came. We looked forward to them. We would hope that our mother would at least make the walk to the store and buy some bread, mac and cheese, spam, pancake mix, rice mixes, hot dogs, Ramen noodles, and a big package of chicken legs. This was the typical shopping list for the first of the month. "Mom's Big Shop," we would call it. A box of mac and cheese would cost about 30 cents and could feed all of us kids. Come to think of it, I don't really remember seeing my mother eat very much. She would split the box of mac and cheese between us and offer each of us a piece of white bread with butter on the side. We were happy to gobble it down.

The food stamps didn't last very long but if we could get Lori to do that initial "Big Shop," we could make it through the month with trips to the food pantry. Lori found a couple of Hispanic women that would buy her food stamps at 50 percent of their value in cash. So $100 in food stamps would get her $50 in cash. Those women would use the stamps to buy their families food. Lori would use the cash to continue the party another night or two. This transaction was no secret to any of us. She made it perfectly clear that this was her money and she was going to do what she wanted with it. I knew that Marie and I could go to the food pantry and bring home some canned goods if we were really hungry. I questioned Lori one time and one time only about the food stamps. I told her that we needed them for food. She had nothing to say. Usually, she had no problem putting me in my place but this time she knew I was right. Still, it didn't change anything. Her addiction had the power. As a child I would blame everyone else but my mother for her actions. She was my mother. We only have one mother and I needed to believe that my mother loved me. She always knew how I felt, everyone did, but we just pushed forward -- one day at a time.

Marie and I would go to the food pantry when we knew it was open. People of all colors and shapes lined up around the building waiting for their turn to walk through the maze-like set up. We pushed our cardboard banana logo boxes along the table as the volunteers asked us how many people were in our family. One woman asked where our mother was. When we told her that our mother was home she just shook her head with disappointment. We knew what she was thinking. We were the only children going through the line without an adult. Marie and I exchanged a supportive look and just continued on. Then, the woman who asked about our mother slipped an extra jar of peanut butter into our box. This filled my heart with excitement! As we carried our loot home, I remember thinking that maybe -- just maybe -- we could make peanut butter cookies. That's just what we did! Lori didn't have to help. The recipe was right on the jar. Marie and I had that covered and we knew she wouldn't make them anyways. I remember dancing around the kitchen as the oven warmed. We took turns measuring and mixing the ingredients. The smells as the cookies began to bake made my mouth water. I knew I would have no self-control when the cookies came out of the oven. These beautiful treats would not last one day in our apartment. That was a good day!

During my time in the projects I often wished I were Hispanic. My Hispanic friends always had a warm pot of rice and beans on the stove. I was instantly made to feel welcome. Their homes were clean and they would clear the living room floor and dance together as a family. Kids were encouraged to join in. Laughter filled the room and I never wanted to leave. They loved me and I loved them. I was accepted and protected in their community. I would even go to church and Sunday school with them on occasion. One of the services I visited was completely in Spanish. I didn't care. It was amazing and I enjoyed every second. I truly believe that this was what saved my childhood.

I knew that in order to survive in the projects I had to be aligned with the Hispanic people. They were the majority. I made friends with the biggest and best of the crew. They taught me how to fight even harder. I could take a punch and I could deliver one without hesitation. I spoke street Spanish well and could hold my own in a conversation. We were the only white family that wasn't having rocks thrown through our windows late at night or bottle rockets put under our door. White families were pushed out of these projects. They were not welcome. I made friends with the right people and so we were protected for the most part. If by chance someone did target my place I would talk to my friends the next day and they would take care of whoever was responsible.

Marisol and Anna were my best friends. Marisol was the youngest of three girls. Anna had an older brother. Anna and I were in the same class. Marisol was two years ahead. Marisol's older sisters were involved with boys from the gang. They were used to seeing me around. Marisol had a life that was a lot more structured than mine. She was the youngest of her siblings and her mother was much older than Lori. Marisol was responsible for cleaning the kitchen every night after dinner. I would help her in return for the amazing food I had enjoyed. She taught me how to dance in her living room. I charmed her family and their friends. Always up for anything, I knew enough to be very respectful. It was important that they liked me because they would then look after me. To me, that was worth more than any amount of money. I knew what happened to the people they didn't care for. Your life would be made miserable. Rocks were thrown through windows. In the middle of the night someone would kick your door as hard as they could and yell, "Get the fuck out of here honkey". Honkey is what white people were called back then by anyone that was not white. I assure you, it was not meant in a nice way. If the people of the projects didn't want you living there you most definitely did not want to be there. I had a false sense of security. Our apartment was rarely a target. If we were targeted it would be taken care of quickly. All I would have to do is tell Marisol or Anna what happened. They would pass it along to her family members and they found a way to get the message across that I was a friend. I guess it is true what they say, "it is all about who you know." Life in the projects could have been a lot worst. I know that now. I knew it back then.

11

Defining Moment #1

As an adult we talk about "defining moments," those times in our lives when we are forced to make a decision that will impact how we navigate our journey. I can vividly recall each important fork in the road in my life -- that moment when time seems to stop. You think to yourself, *Holy shit, how did I get here and where do I go from here?* You stop and think about your options. You feel like your life is about to change in a significant way no matter how you choose but, you have to make a choice and that choice will determine which way your journey, your path, leads you. Fight or flight kicks in.

I have had a few of these moments but one in particular was the most defining. I have never been as scared as I was this one night. At the age of 13, I was forced to run out of my friend's family's apartment at 2 a.m. and run over a mile to my apartment, to my mother, to my family, for safety.

Marisol was having a sleepover at her older sister's apartment. I was there along with another girl and we were up late watching movies. The apartment had two bedrooms and a pullout couch. But it didn't really matter because on these overnights we always found a place with a blanket to fall asleep. The bonus this night was a fantastic pot of rice and beans on the stove that was free for the taking. There was really no one person telling us what to do. We were respectful of the house and in return Marisol's family would let us come for sleepovers almost every weekend. I never had them at my house. I knew better than to do that.

This apartment was at the far end of the projects. Marisol's older sister had a young daughter that I knew well. She was no more than four years old, an adorable little girl that I played with often. She would dance with us in the living room and sing to us with her pretend microphone. She was absolutely precious! This particular night she was having trouble falling asleep. She came into the living room rubbing her eyes and sobbing. Her mother was already in bed. I want to say her mother was pregnant but I am not 100 percent. Her father was sitting at the kitchen table drinking. She gave me the biggest hug and I put her on my lap, rocking my legs side to side to make her smile. It was too late for her to be up. I let her stay for a while but then told her that I would lay with her if she agreed to go back to bed. She was an only child and had her own room. We said goodnight to everyone and I brought her to her room. I curled up next to her and we both fell asleep around midnight. I was relieved for the excuse to leave the movie. I was absolutely exhausted and fell asleep within just a few minutes of lying with my little friend. Her stuffed animals surrounded me. This made me smile. I never had stuffed animals. None that I can remember that is. Nothing that was special to me. I still sleep with my arms wrapped around myself. I imagine this is how I put myself to sleep when I was younger.

We slept for about an hour when the door opened and I heard someone come into the room. I didn't move. I convinced myself it was my friend looking for a place to sleep. Suddenly, a large person lay down next to me in the bed. My back was facing the door. I could smell alcohol on his breath. It was Marisol's uncle, the little girl's father. His name is lost to me. He had black curly hair, big puffy lips, and a round face. He was not a tall man, but not a short man either. He defiantly enjoyed eating. His body was round and plump. His hands were puffy and his fingers like sausages. He wore a gold chain around his neck and rings on his fingers. He spoke mostly in Spanish but knew some broken English. Between my street Spanish and his broken English we always seemed to be able to communicate. I had had many sleepovers at his family's house. I adored his daughter. I played with her often. I danced in their living room. I ate their food. I cleaned their house, grateful to be able to escape from my own home. I was one of them until this night. Until this moment.

He spoke to me softly in Spanish. He told me that I was beautiful. I felt his disgusting hot breath on my neck and his fat stomach pushed up against my back. He started to rub my arm. I didn't move. I was curled into his daughter as tightly as I could be. I couldn't move. I didn't want to wake her. I didn't want to scare her. I didn't want to hurt her. I couldn't move.

I could hear the television playing in the other room. I knew my friends where still up. I wondered what they were thinking. They must have seen him come in. They knew he had been drinking all night and that he had been in this room too long. It's not like he came in to get a blanket and then left. He came in to lie next to me. How could they not know? How could they not come in? How could they not protect me? I was scared and I was paralyzed. I knew what he wanted and I didn't know how to get out. This precious little girl was fast asleep in front of me and I couldn't wake her. I couldn't let her see her father like this. He pulled my pants and underwear down from behind. I didn't move. He pulled his pants down enough to pull his penis out. I didn't move. He kissed my neck. I didn't move. He tried to push himself inside me. I stayed still. I was a virgin. I was small. I was untouched. He began to hurt me. I knew that if I didn't leave that instant, if I didn't risk waking this precious little girl, I was never going to be the same. It came to me quickly. If I touched her, she would move a little and it would scare him. I grabbed her under her arm and gently squeezed. She moved. He froze. I sat up quickly and jumped out of bed. I pulled my pants up and reached for the door. I rushed out into the living room blinded by the light of the television. My "friends" were all sitting on the couch. Someone asked where I was going. I put on my shoes and bolted down the three flights of stairs. No one stopped me. No one even stood up from the couch. No one asked me what had happened.

I ran all the way home. I ran to 15 B. It was dark and I was scared shitless! There were people sitting on their stoops in the shadows. There were hookers. There were druggies. There were monsters. I didn't care. I had to run. I had to get home. I ran into the back hallway because that was the closest way in. I knew not to look around. I just needed to get to my door. I banged on the door until Lori opened it. She looked at me with a blank stare as I ran inside. Suddenly, I felt relief. I knew I was safe now, but I also knew I was not the same.

Lori never asked me where I had been. She never asked me why I had come home. She never questioned the petrified look on my face. She just told me to go to bed and so I did just that. I went to bed but I couldn't sleep; my mind was racing. Everything had changed now. I no longer trusted my friends. I no longer had an escape from my house. What in the hell was I supposed to do now? I showered in the morning for at least an hour. I told myself that I was still a virgin because he didn't make it in. I was still good. I was still clean.

That next day I knew what I had to do. I had to move to Jackson, Maine and live with my father and Marie. I had to get the hell out of Great Brook Valley. I called my father that day. I told him that I needed to move with him. He and my mother had always told us that when we were at least 11 years old that we would be able to decide where we wanted to live. We would be old enough then. I told him that I was getting into trouble and that I was afraid that I would ruin my life. I begged him to come and get me.

Lori didn't question my motive. She knew that the Valley was not safe for a young girl. At least I tell myself that she knew. When I told her I was leaving she didn't ask me to stay. She didn't ask me how I knew for sure this time. She spoke to me as if I were an adult making an adult decision. She just told me "if that's what you want". That was the end of the discussion. I cannot wrap my head around what she was thinking at the time. My hope is that she knew that I would have a fighting chance if I got out of the projects. She let me go because she knew it was the right thing to do. The reality of it all is, she didn't have a choice.

It was about two weeks later that I was on my way to Maine. While waiting for my father to arrive, I stayed close to home. I never spoke to any of those people again. I wondered what Marisol's uncle had said to them about why I had run out. How had he explained the terrified look on my face? What story did he tell his family, his wife, to excuse what he had done? How did he explain why he came into that room in the first place? I have to trust that Marisol knows the truth and that she chose her family because it was all that she had. I chose myself because it was all that I had.

Marie was so happy to have me with her again. She was excited to share her room with me. We spoke on the phone at length. I didn't tell her what had happened. I didn't have to. She could hear it in my voice. I had waivered back and forth over the past two years trying to decide if I wanted to move to Maine or if I would stay in Massachusetts and be a "city girl". There was no longer a question. My father and Marie knew I meant it. I didn't care who my father was living with at the time. He had been married and divorced two times. He was now onto the third live in girlfriend. I knew I could make it work. I had to make it work.

12

Jackson, Maine - The Big Move

Up until I was 11, I would spend about a month in Maine with my father and his family

every summer. We would get a taste of the country life. Our last name was Dodge,

"like the truck" I used to say. Marie and I would travel to Jackson, Maine to visit with our

father and the Dodge side of the family. My father had a small beef cattle farm. It was

a quarter mile down the road from my grandfather's large dairy farm, which had been in

the family for several generations. The farm consisted of over 300 acres of land. It did

not have a real monetary value, since land was cheap in Jackson. Today, you can buy

an acre of land for around two thousand dollars or less. I can only imagine what it was

over 30 years ago.

The main farmhouse was yellow. It is grey now; the paint has mostly worn away. The

house itself has hardwood floors, five bedrooms and a glassed-in porch that my

grandfather turned into his work area. He built a large workbench and always had a

project he was working on. Most of our toys were homemade. Behind the main house

were several small buildings that included a working sawmill that could cut large boards

for building, and a garage to store snowmobiles and four-wheelers. Attached to the

house was a woodshed leading to a chicken coop and a long hallway that would take

you into the large barn, which could hold about 50 cows at a time for milking. I loved

the smell of the barn. Hay was stacked to the ceiling on the second floor and there was

a basement level as well that held small animals and supplies. My grandfather did not

mess around. He had a working farm and he worked hard until he was in his 80s.

We were allowed to help feed the animals even as small children. My grandfather loved watching us interact with them. I loved his pigs. Not only were they hilarious, but I could also tell that they were intelligent creatures. I remember thinking as a child that they were as smart as dogs but because they smell and eat smelly food we couldn't let them into our house. This still makes me smile. I have toy pigs in my office. The students get a kick out of playing with them. When someone makes a police reference I just smile and say, "Funny right." This always gets a laugh.

The farm was a great place to be as a child. My grandparents were loving and patient. They were exactly how I want to be when I have grandchildren one day.

Jackson is a small town with one main route running through it. The closest gas station and food mart from our house was eight miles away. We did not even have our own post office. The population was just about two thousand. We had a small community church most people only visited during the holidays. There was a small community center as well. This was the place the community came together for celebrations or any event really. It was centrally located and held BINGO nights as well as Friday night dances for our little town. Every holiday season they community members held a craft fair. I loved to walk around and admire all of the homemade treasures. I never had a penny in my pocket. That didn't matter. It was fun to see what the Jackson women had come up with. I loved the smell of the cinnamon sticks and Christmas treasures.

My Uncle Paul lives in between the two farms in a regular house that he built with his own hands. He had two sons and a daughter with his first wife. My cousins lived with their mother for most of their childhood so we didn't see them too often. Uncle Paul is a hard workingman. I would put him in the same category as Aunt Maggie. He has always been supportive and loving to Marie and I. He has a small engine repair shop, and has worked on all of the locals' four-wheelers and snowmobiles. In Jackson just about everyone had either one or the other. If you were lucky you had both.

On the other end of the road was my Aunt Mary. She had two daughters that were just a little older than me. It was nice having cousins up the road to play with. Aunt Mary was married to a man named Lester. "Lester the Molester" was what we called him. He was a nasty, dirty little man. He stood no higher than five feet tall. He had an evil soul and you could feel it. Having had the experiences I had in the Valley I knew exactly what Lester was all about. I had a pit in my stomach every time I was around him. I told Marie to never allow herself to be alone with that man. My street smarts had taught me one very valuable lesson. I could smell a predator a mile away. My cousins didn't have a choice. I don't know how my cousins survived living with that man. It was no secret that he was a bad man and he hurt young girls. My father made it very clear that we were not allowed around him and if he ever even came near us he would kill him. "Lester the Molester" knew this and knew better. Anyone this man touched has struggled their whole life. As for my aunt I have no idea what fantasy world she was living in. I know her daughters told her about his late night visits to their room. She dismissed their clams immediately. She told other family members that the girls were making it up. They were angry teenage girls. They wanted to do whatever they wished without consequences. They wanted Lester out of the house because he was too strict.

She sold this to our family members and she sold it to herself. The worst part is everyone stood by and watched the destruction of two beautiful young girls. Marie and I stood up for the girls to show them our support. Lester found out about my verbal rant of what a pig he was. The very next day Marie and I were told that we were no longer allowed to visit our cousins at their house. We would only be able to see them at school. I knew it was coming. I knew Lester was afraid of what we may say or do to get the word out. He decided to isolate the girls from us. My aunt allowed this. The girls no longer had an outlet. They were trapped and isolated in that house with that man. The girls left the house as soon as they could. Their innocence left behind them. It would take years for their scars to heal. Mary finally snapped out of it and left him. Unfortunately, she waited until her daughters were already grown. Lester died of cancer just a few years after she left him. No one from our family attended his funeral.

The Dodge road had a lot to be desired. It was a long dirt road running through acres of pasture land and small country houses. The homes were mainly built with the owners bare hands. Board by board, nail by nail. They didn't hire contractors to build their homes. Friends and family members came together, combining their skills and built the homes. The Dodge road had a lot of different characters living on it. In a way this was similar to the Valley. There were safe places and not so safe places. Our Uncle Paul's home was safe. Aunt Mary's house was clearly not safe. As young children Marie and I were sheltered in Jackson. Our grandmother Doris was our main caretaker. She kept us close by her side during our summer visits to Maine. We slept and ate all of our meals with her at the farm. She was the reason we were able to visit our father. He was not in any position to be looking after children back in those days. My father was on and off with relationships and did not have room or the ability to look after us. He was a jack-of-all-trades and worked as many jobs as he could. He had built a small shack at the time and it was not a place for small children. There was a wood stove, but no running water or bathroom. Eventually, he added electricity and a well.

My grandfather Lawrence was born and raised on this farm. He only went away to serve in WWII and returned to marry my grandmother Doris. At the time, Doris was 15 years old and Lawrence was 30. Doris had three children by the time she was twenty-one and raised them all on that farm. She only left the farm she was with my grandfather. She was liberated in her 40s, when she was finally allowed to get her driver's license. At this time, she was helping to raise her other grandchildren. My grandparents did not have a lot of money but what we did have was plenty of food. Grandma Doris had a large garden filled with delicious vegetables. These were a delicacy for Marie and me. During the time that we were there I would stand in the bean aisle and eat green beans until I couldn't eat anymore. I remember my grandmother just laughing as we picked. She would say, "Fill your belly but then you have to fill your bucket and bring them in." I was happy to help out. I loved the feeling of the sun on my face and the snap of the fresh beans in my mouth. I also loved walking up and down the fields. The smell of the grass and the dirt. The sight of the animals in the pasture following me along the fence line. My grandparents were a gift to my life.

The freezer was filled with beef from one of my father's cows. My grandmother made everything from scratch. We had three square meals a day. As we got older we definitely earned those meals. The summer months were spent "haying," mowing and baling the hay fields. After the bailing was completed we would ride on the back of a huge hay trailer and pick up and stack the hay. This was no easy task, but it was a necessary evil. We needed enough hay for the long Maine winter. We would start haying around 8:00 a.m. and finish in the late afternoon. Sometimes we would be out in the fields until dark trying to beat a storm.

My grandfather had at least 100 dairy cows and my father averaged about 50 beef cows. The dairy cows had to be milked twice a day, once in early morning and then again in the early evening. Beef cows are raised for their meat. They are not typically milked.

Summers were my favorite time of year. We got away from the city and ran the fields. We adapted to the farm life as well as we adapted to the city life. It was what we knew. Marie and I definitely craved the farm life. Everything we needed was there. Life was simple. My grandmother would even make some of their clothes. It was definitely "The Way Life Should Be." So many times I wished that my parents had stayed together so that I could have been raised on the farm.

My father married his second wife Sherry when I was around nine years old. This was great for my father. She was kind and loving and he was very happy. They met when they were both working at a chicken factory in Belfast, Maine. He left his pregnant girlfriend Deborah for Sherry. She was divorced, with two sons – Eddie (16 years old) and Jeffrey (nine, the same age as me). With Sherry in the picture, we could stay with him during our summer months. While we visited, Sherry looked after Marie and me as if we were her own children. Marie was just turning 11 and so this was when she made the move to Maine from Massachusetts. Sherry was not a fan of the farm life. I believe that she enjoyed the outdoors; I just don't think manual labor was something she wanted to do on her off time. She would complain about the farming and say they lived too far away from anything. This is funny to me because this is the same issue that Lori had with Jackson, Maine. That marriage only lasted a couple of years. Sherry wanted to go back to Belfast and live near people and places.

I was close with her son Jeffrey since we were the same age. He was a cute boy and we would say that if our parents were not married we would be married. It was a sweet little crush. Better than that, he liked to climb trees and was up for just about anything so I gravitated towards him. His older brother Eddie was a different story.

Eddie was a pothead; in fact, he grew his own on my father's land. He also used to sniff gasoline for a quick high. He told me to try it one time. I just started coughing and told him I thought sniffing gas was one of the stupidest things you could do. He never asked me to do this again. Eddie was tall and skinny, with short brown hair and some acne. He was what I would consider a smart ass. He thought he was cool, and he walked around like he was in charge when my father wasn't nearby. He gave me the creeps, especially when he would watch me. When I looked at him, he would give a half smile and I could see his nasty green teeth. It was clear that he had not seen a dentist in a very long time. He wore dirty, grease-stained clothes and didn't seem to care about his appearance. His fingernails were always black underneath. I remember he took a bar of soap into the water when we went swimming one time. He came out of the water and he was still dirty. It would take more than a bar of soap to wash his filth away. I didn't like Eddie from day one. I knew that there was something wrong with him. This was another instance in my life that I wish I had known enough to listen to my instincts. My instincts were always right.

Eddie liked to sneak into my bed at night when everyone else was sleeping. He hurt me more times than I can count. At first I said "no," and told him to "get out of my room." He wouldn't stop. I wrapped myself in blankets as tight as I could. It didn't matter. He never gave up. His hands were cold and strong. I couldn't fight him off. I know that he had done this to my sister as well. Eddie would threaten to tell my father something that I had done, or even worse, he would make something up. Looking back now, I am sure it was something ridiculous and at best I would have gotten a swat on my ass but at the time I was petrified of having my father mad at me. I didn't want to be sent back to Massachusetts too soon. I didn't want my father to look at me differently. I craved his approval and his love.

At first Eddie would just touch me and ask me to touch him. Each time he came in he would go a little further. Push me further. I wanted to hurt him. I wanted to bite him. I wanted to kill him. I never did anything. Now I felt dirty, as if what had happened was my fault. I didn't want my father or anyone else to think I was dirty. I figured out that if we were going to be home alone I had better go visit my grandmother. I avoided Eddie, and eventually he stopped coming to me. I was always nervous around him. I can't believe that no one ever picked up on this. I can tell in an instant when my children are anxious or upset. How did my feelings go unnoticed? Was I that good of an actress or was no one paying attention? I never told anyone about Eddie, certainly not my father. I wish that I had. I know now that he would have done something about it. I am not sure if Marie knew what was going on with Eddie and me. I imagine that she did. I couldn't think about it. I never looked at Marie as someone that would protect me. I was always the one looking out for her. I was never angry with Marie for being silent. I understood that this was who she was. It was my job to be outspoken and strong. That was who I was. Marie did eventually tell our father about her experiences with Eddie but not until after they moved away. Sherry left my father to move back to Belfast a year after Marie had moved to Maine. She found another man that mad her happy. My father was devastated. He was always the one doing the leaving. He had lost the "love of his life" or so he said. As for Eddie, I know that after my father and Sherry divorced, Eddie was in and out of jail. He was living in Belfast and we would hear about something that he had done to land him in jail. He liked to break into people's houses when they weren't home. I am sure it was to buy drugs. I hate Eddie. When I think of him I get very angry. People like Eddie belong in Prison. If I look at it from a healing point I can say that the experiences I have had with Eddie have helped me to understand where assault victims are coming from. I have been there. Sometimes I wish I could tell them that I really do understand. It is important that they know this. I am carful with my words. Up until this point, these have been my secrets. I hope to grow by sharing them.

My father needed time to collect himself after Sherry left. The marriage had ended by the time I move to Maine. The only time I spent with Sherry was during my summer visits. It was about a year after she left that I made that desperate phone call begging for my father to come and get me. I was sad that she was not going to be there. She was always nice to me. When she was there we could stay at my fathers small house instead of at the farm. I loved the farm, but I loved my father more. I craved time with him. When my father came to get me for the big move I had a couple of bags of my favorite things and that was it. I threw my stuff into the trunk of my father's car and jumped in quickly so that my father couldn't change his mind. I left everything and everyone else behind, including Andrew and Jessie. I felt terrible about leaving them but I knew that I had to make this change for myself and that this was the time to do it. I know that they understand now but at the time I know they were heartbroken. Andrew cried when I left and I cried for both of them. I am not sure how my mother reacted but I knew that she would be lost without me. She would now be on her own with the kids. She was not seeing anyone special at this time and so it would all fall back on her. In less than a month after I left, my mother moved from the projects to live closer to Dave for the sake of the kids. They stayed with Dave for a while but that didn't work out for very long. Dave was living with his mother Maxine and she did not like Lori. Maxine kicked Lori out after a couple of months. She didn't like Lori crawling home from the bar and waking up the whole house. Lori ended up in a shelter with the kids for a while until she could save up enough money to get her own place. This was not a bad move for Lori. It made her responsible because she had no other choice than to be. She knew that in order to avoid getting kicked out of the shelter, she wouldn't be able to drink on site. She also knew enough not to come back to the shelter so drunk that she'd get into fights with the other people there. These restrictions motivated Lori to save money and get her own place. She wanted her freedom again.

After Sherry left my father, he went back to Deborah. This is the same Deborah that my father had left for Sherry. She was pregnant when he left her, but now she had a young son. My father's son. My father couldn't be alone. My father also loved his children. This was an easy decision for him. Deborah was still in love with my father. She took him back without hesitation. Marie was living in the house during this transition period. I can't imagine what that was like. I know one thing for sure. She was excited for me to join her. We would have the upstairs loft area for our bedroom. Our beds were old army cots at first. I got a "real" mattress before Marie; she had to wait a lot longer for hers. I am not really sure how that whole thing worked out. Most of the house was unfinished. There was no sheetrock, just a cement slab floor, particle board, and insulation. We used to peer through the cracks in the walls to see what was going on outside. The upstairs was not wired for electricity and so we ran extension cords up through the entrance hole. We used a ladder to go up and down into our room. We did have two windows on the back wall of our room and the chimney to the woodstove went through our room, which kept us warm. The chimney made a huge difference for the cold winters. We also had old army wool blankets to go with the army cots. My father must have picked them up at an auction; he loved going to auctions and bringing home this type of stuff. He did make sure that we had what we needed. He used to tell us, "As soon as I have enough money, I'm going to finish that room." To this day, the room is still not finished.

We didn't have a home phone for a long time. It would just be another bill my father would have to pay. He believed that you should never spend more than you had, and so he carried all the cash that he had in his pocket. No credit cards, no loans. He didn't even have a loan to build his house. He bought everything that he needed as we went along. Every car or truck that he owned he paid cash for. He was definitely old school in many ways -- and I do not mean that as a compliment.

My father also believed that men should be in charge of finances and all "major responsibilities" and women should not own land. He was more than happy to have his wife stay home and take care of the kids. My father looked up to his father in many ways –in terms of the farming and maintaining control. As he got older, he relaxed the reins. He seemed to roll with the daily managing of our household. He allowed Deborah to go out more with her friends. He was calmer. The only exception I would make to this is in the exception of money. If Deborah, or his two ex-wives wanted money; they would have to ask for it and explain why they needed it. There was no 50/50 split. He was the major decision maker because he was the man of the house making all of the money.

Roles were very clear for my father but not so much for Marie and me. We would take care of food preparation and cleaning, but then we would do the farming and lug the wood. I was always bitter about the double standard. We would serve everyone their plates at dinnertime and then go back and make our own. After everyone ate we would go around and pick their plates up and do the dishes. I always thought that this was unfair and too much for two girls in high school. We had already done the farming chores and the dinner chores and at some point we had to get our homework done. While everyone else was watching *America's Funniest Home Videos*, we were at the table getting our work done. This was the way of life whether my father was home or not.

Where was Deborah when this was all happening? She was sitting comfortably in her chair waiting for her meal to be served. Occasionally, my father would speak up and ask her why she wasn't helping. This would cause WWIII and it just was not worth it. Deborah would go on a tirade about how much she does and how my father is never home. She would say that he didn't appreciate her and that she needed a break. Deborah was a yeller. She would yell at the top of her lungs. Her voice would cut right through you. We all knew that she was not going to stop until she got her way. Eventually, my father would give in and just leave it be. Marie and I had it covered anyways. We knew not to complain about it. If we did, it would come back to haunt us tenfold and it was just not worth it.

Deborah is a whole story on her own. She had her first child at 13 years old. She had her second son when she was 16 or 17 and then a third son with my father. Three boys, three different fathers. My father and Deborah's sons name was Michael. Michael is about six years younger than me. Everyone knew that my father always wanted a son. It was not something he kept secret. Knowing how my father felt about boys and having a son, Deborah knew that Michael was her ticket to the farm. She had come from a very poor family and struggled her entire life. My father offered her security, a home, and living on a farm where she knew she would never go hungry. According to her family, Deborah had told them that my father was rich or at least he would be one day when he took over my grandfather's larger farm. The plan was always for my father to take over the farmhouse after my grandparents were gone. He would continue his family tradition and continue to farm the beautiful land.

Everything was self-contained on the farm. My grandparents even had a large safe that would hold anything valuable; especially large amounts of cash that would come in the fall when my father would sell off any young bulls that needed selling before breeding cows. There was no need for banks. No need for "those people" to know how much money we have. Who those people were, I have no idea.

My father would sell off the bulls because it was important not to allow inbreeding and it gave our family funds that would support us through the winter when work was hard to find. Some winters, my father would work straight through and others he would have a couple of months off to just focus on his farm. I loved it when he was home. I felt safe and protected, at least when he was home. Deborah seemed to keep herself in check. I loved my father more than anything, despite some of his choices. He never tried to hurt me or put me in harm's way. He did the best that he could with what he had. He made choices just like we all do and some of them were better than others. Now that we were in Maine, our lives had changed completely. I personally knew that this was the best-case scenario for a very shitty situation. I had no interest in going back to Massachusetts unless it was for a visit with the kids. They were the only pull I felt when thinking about that life. I thought about them often. I thought about them living in a

shelter with my mother. I thought about them searching for food to eat. I thought about

the terrible things they were probably witnessing. I knew that they were not being cared

for. I was no longer there to make sure they had clean clothes and baths before bed. I

didn't trust Lori with them. Lori brought Marie and I to Bars when we were their ages. I

knew at the very least the kids would find themselves unsafe and feeling anxious. They

were so young when I left them. They were still sweet and innocent. Would they be

able to handle what was inevitably coming their way? I could not longer protect them.

To this day I still wonder if I could have helped them more. If only I could have

managed just a few more years to guide them through their adolescent years. I could

have stuck up for them and protected them. I am still looking for answers to these

questions. Perhaps I should consider trying to forgive myself for leaving them. We are

our own worst critic right?

Transitions are never easy. I was carrying a heavy load on my back. When I needed

to calm my mind I found piece in pastures of Jackson, Maine. I would walk the fields

and wonder the woods. I wondered lost deep inside of my own thoughts. I had guilt. I

had regret. I had pain. More than of this I had love for myself. I had to believe that I

had made the right choice because I loved myself.

My new life had a new set of rules. In chess I always tell my children that we have to be

thinking three steps ahead. My new life was a completely different match. I had to

figure out the game and how to play it to my full advantage. My father's house was not the safe country home I dreamt it could be. Deborah was there now. Sherry was gone. Deborah had a temper. She was quick to raise her hand when parenting. It wasn't long before I figured out this new life was going to be very challenging, but I had made my choice. I was going to have to learn to live with it.

13

Everything Changes but Not for the Better

Now that I had moved to Maine, my schedule would be reversed. I would be in Maine for the school year and go to Massachusetts for at least a month in the summer. Marie and I were together again. We were now on the same schedule and would visiting Lori and the kids during the summer months. By the time our first summer visit came, Lori had her own apartment. It was really cute and she kept it nice and clean. Andrew had his own room, which he absolutely loved. Jessie was in a walk-in closet. Literally. It was actually perfect for her, since she was a peanut. There was enough room for her bed and a few toys; the problem was, her closet was in Lori's room. I can only imagine the things that Jessie was exposed to sharing a bedroom with my mother. Actually, I didn't have to imagine, I already knew.

When I first saw Lori's new apartment in Athol, I thought perhaps she was getting her shit together. This thought flew by rather quickly as we began to spend time together. She was right back to her old tricks by the second week Marie and I were there. It started with her saying she was going to get milk and then she returned almost two hours later. When we asked why it took so long, she just said she needed a walk. We knew that she had snuck in for a quick pop and probably got to chatting with one of her "friends." Each time she did this, she would be gone for a little bit longer, as if testing her boundaries. Had she forgotten that she was our mother? Marie and I knew that we were more responsible but this made me worry about the kids when we were gone.

What happened to them then? I told myself that Dave would probably come and take them and that they would be fine. I had to tell myself that.

There was a new guy coming around. His name was John, and he was one of those people that instantly gave you a bad feeling. The hair on the back of my neck stood up, my stomach would feel off. Everything in my body told me to stay away from this guy. I was starting to get really good at recognizing these feelings for what they were and actually listening to them. He was always staring at my breasts. He watched me too long, especially when my mother was out of the room. I was more concerned about Jessie than myself. Even though he creeped me out on more than one occasion, I knew that I could handle him. Lucky for him he never went too far.

John had another side to him. He was violent and abusive with or without alcohol. He thought it was a sport to beat on my mother. As many fights as my mother had with Dave, he never punched her just to punch her. He fought her off, for sure, but he never punched her in the face for sport. Lori had at least four black eyes that I know of, never mind the bruises all over her body. She was becoming someone I didn't recognize. She was a battered woman. I could see she was tired of fighting and she had stopped fighting back. She was also afraid of being alone. This was never an issue in Worcester. Lori never had a problem finding a fill-in boyfriend when she needed one. Now she was in a small town and the pickings were slim. It took about two years but John finally went to jail for an extended stay after beating my mother one too many times. Lori refused to press charges or to make a statement to the police but that didn't matter. The laws were changing to support women in this situation and thank God that

105

they did because I think he would have eventually killed her. The state would be the one pressing the charges and they had built a case strong enough over the several beatings to put him away. This forced my mother to face the truth about the relationship and she eventually moved on from it.

By the end of our summer vacation, Lori was really comfortable and would ask us to watch the kids and she would disappear in the bar for the day, making it home just in time for bedtime. We could not have cared less what she was doing or whom she was doing it with. Marie and I cared about seeing the kids more than spending time with her at this point. We took them to the lake and the playgrounds. We took them to any place they wanted to go that was within walking distance. We had as much fun as they did. Andrew would wake up every morning with a full smile on his face. "Jamie, are we going on another adventure today?" I would always tell him "but of course handsome boy." I could never say NO to those big blue eyes. Jesse was easy to please. All we would have to say is grab your shoes and she would jump around like a little puppy excited to play. For those few weeks in the summer, they were allowed to just be kids and so were we. Lori didn't supervise anything that we did. There really wasn't any kind of trouble to get into in Athol. We didn't know anyone anyway and all we wanted to do was spend time with the kids. I did happen to find a babysitting job for a neighbor. There was a single mother with two boys living in the first floor apartment. She was desperate for a night out. She offered to do a perm in my hair if I watched the boys for a couple of nights. For some reason I thought I really wanted a perm. This was not one of my better beauty decisions. I looked like a standard poodle with long blond hair.

Despite the perm, I did enjoy the time I spent babysitting her boys. They were sweet and fun to play around with. I was happy to know I was helping out their mom.

Marie and I made it through those summers unharmed. We were with the kids from sun up to sun down. I slept with Andrew in his room and Marie slept on the couch. We had some great times with Dave as well. He had gone to school to become a Certified Nurse's Assistant, which was no easy task for someone that had been out of school for over 20 years. He created a new life for himself and got a job working at a hospital. When he wasn't busy working, Dave was happy to take all of us kids to places a little further away. We were thrilled to go to a drive-in theater that he loved. It was almost as if we were living like a normal family, even if was just for a day. Dave also brought over groceries occasionally to make sure we all had food. This gave me comfort. Their life was better here in Athol than it had been in the projects. No more crazy parties with strangers coming over to the house (well, at least none I knew of). Instead, Lori went out to the bars. We could sleep through the night without having to call the police.

A week before the next round of food stamps came in, Marie and I realized that we were getting low on food. Even with Dave's help we managed to run out. Marie and I went right into action, and walked over to the Salvation Army office, which was just down the road from Lori's apartment. We told them that we were running out of food and we needed help. Marie stood by my side while I did most of the talking. I put on my pouting face and went for it.

"We have five people in our family. Our mother is a single mother of four. We are out of milk and bread and our cupboards are bare. Can't you help us? We just need enough to get by the next week."

The words seemed to roll off of my tong. The woman asked where our mother was and why she had sent two children alone. I repeated the story that I had told so many times before, that our mother was sick and so she couldn't come on her own. This office was run by a married couple and was much smaller than the one in Worcester. They were not as accustomed to people coming in off the street and asking for food. I didn't care about that. I was going to provide for my family. They put together two bags of food for us to bring home. They told us that we could only come back once a month. I made sure to pass that along to Lori even though I knew she would never go on her own.

One day, around noontime, I noticed Lori was shaking badly. I knew that she had not had anything to drink yet and her body was craving it. She had told us that she didn't have any money to go out. She did have a single roll of quarters that was for the laundry. It had piled up and we were planning on going that day. I took Marie aside and asked her what she thought about doing the laundry by hand in the bathtub so that mom could go out. This was something that we used to do in the Valley and it really wasn't that difficult. Lori was getting irritable and we would all have a better day if she went out. Marie hesitated but then went along with my plan. She knew that I was right and that Lori's shakes would only get worse and then we would all feel the wrath of her irritability. I knew that I had to do whatever I could to avoid an explosion. I knew that as long as Lori was able to go to the bar we would all be able to make it through the night.

When Lori was irritable there was not telling what would trigger an angry rage. She loved to throw furniture or "warm your ass" if you got into her way. This was the right thing to do for all of us. I had to take control of the situation. Marie and I walked out into the living room together and I presented my option to my mother. I told her that we were happy to wash the laundry in the tub so that she could go out. She didn't even hesitate. Lori instantly beamed and grabbed the coins and she was off. She didn't come home for several hours. She knew how to stretch a buck or a quarter in this case. We made the most of this day with the kids. Marie wasn't thrilled about washing the clothes. I decided I had better just do it. I filled the tub with hot water and asked her to keep an eye on the kids. On my hand and knees I scrubbed the clothes. Marie and Andrew helped wring out the clothes so they could be hung outside to dry. My hands were wrinkled and sore by the time we were done. I finished as quickly as I could. I was as excited as the kids were for our days adventure. Marie packed up Andrew and Jesse and we headed out to the park.

When Lori came home late that night I made sure the kids were already in bed. She managed to stretch that roll of quarters for a few hours. It was impressive. She was drunk off of her ass. Struggling to put the key into the door. I got up and opened the door. She thanked me. I told her that the laundry was done and the kids were in bed. "Thanks kid." Slurred out of her mouth. "Mom, you should probably go lay down." Lori's face changed as she became instantly angry. "Don't you fucking tell me what to do." I knew enough to back off. Lori did not like anyone telling her what to do. I backed away and went to bed in Andrews' room. Lori passed out on the couch and everyone else got a good night sleep. It was about two weeks later we returned to Maine. The kids always cried when we left. I didn't blame them. My guilt for leaving them returned but honestly I couldn't wait to go back to Maine. I only wished I could bring them with me.

14

Red

We called Deborah "Red" because of her dyed, bright-red hair and because of her famous temper. Even when she bleached it blonde, we still called her Red. The name fit. Regardless of the color of her hair, it was always pulled up high on her head in a banana clip. She looked like one of the people in the Wal-Mart jokes online. She was not a very attractive woman. She had beady eyes and her body type reminded me of humpty dumpty, round on top with skinny little legs. She always had a bitter look on her face. Her lips were pressed tightly together and it was extremely rare to see her smile or laugh. Everything was serious to her. She thought everyone was out to get her. Red was famous for wearing spandex. I am not a fan of spandex but she loved it. She would buy the brightest colors she could find and wear them proudly. During the summer months, she would wear just a sports bra with her spandex shorts. Her belly would stand out large, scarred with deep stretch marks from her pregnancies. The worst part was the camel toe in her crotch that you could not help but stare at. Red had no business wearing these tight shorts but I knew enough not to be the one to tell her.

Red struggled with substance abuse as well. Her drugs of choice were prescription pills. She had several doctors in different counties of Maine that she would rotate through to get her prescriptions filled. This was no secret to any of us. The only time she relaxed was if she was high. We knew when she had taken one pill too many because she would be sitting in her chair with an inch-long ash hanging of the end of her cigarette and broken ashes running down her shirt. She would be staring off into space; what we in law enforcement call going "on the nod," which basically means

111

drifting in and out of consciousness. She would be talking one minute with her cigarette flopping in her lips as she spoke, and then the next minute her head would slump and then she'd pass out. I was waiting for the day that we would come home from school and the house would be burned down from her cigarettes. Her chair had at least 20 to 30 burn holes from her cigarette falling out of her mouth when she blacked out.

I mentioned that Red had three sons. Her second boy Rick was about four years younger than me. He was a very large kid even when he was younger. He is now morbidly obese. Rick made living in the house even more unbearable. He was a pervert and Deborah protected him. He was constantly touching himself in front of us. He would sit on the couch and pull a blanket over his lap so that he could play with himself. He didn't care. I walked in on him on more than one occasion having his way with himself on the living room couch. On those occasions he did not have a cover over his lap. He had absolutely no respect for anyone else in the house or for privacy. I would tell my father about it and Red always said she would "deal with it" but it never stopped and eventually his behavior got worse.

Our bathroom did not have a door. I was told that the pipes would freeze if we closed a door) so instead we had a twin-sized bed sheet hanging in the doorframe. It was held up with thumbtacks. The sheet was old with a variety of holes in it. Rick would stand outside of the sheet, just off to the side where we couldn't see him, and watch us shower. I would scream at him when I did catch him. Red would just tell him to go to his room. This did not just happen a couple of times, it was a constant issue. I hated even going into the bathroom because I knew as soon as I got into the shower he would find his way over to the door. Marie and I started to keep watch for one another. When Marie would shower I would sit at the table and do my work right outside of the bathroom. She would then return the favor. Just when we thought we had it covered and Rick could no longer spy on us we realized that he had moved to the living room, which had a straight-shot view through the window into the bathroom right where the shower stall stood. The shower was one of those cheap, plastic, temporary shower stalls. We couldn't get away from him.

Rick also had an obsession with our underwear. Marie and I noticed that we were running out of underwear. We would check the laundry and there were none to be found. We couldn't figure out where they had all gone. We began to search everywhere for them. Finally, we found them: they were hidden under Rick's bed, and were covered in bodily fluid and his feces. Marie and I made sure to tell my father about this as well. Once again he told Red to take care of it and once again nothing ever changed. Looking back now, I realize that Rick had some serious issues. He is not part of my family. I do not have room in my life for him.

My father overlooked many of Deborah's flaws. He wanted his son. I knew what I was getting myself into when I decided to move to Maine. I knew all about Deborah and what she was capable of. I knew that she could be violent. I knew that she could be cruel. I knew that she was unable to tell the truth. I knew all of this, still I chose Maine because I believed I had a shot to make it. I just needed to get through school and get out on my own.

For the most part, Marie and I were able to stay out of Deborah's way. As long as we did what she said, everything was fine. That was until my father got a "chance of a lifetime" and went to New York City for a job working with a crew on the George Washington Bridge. His friend Dan came to the house one night and told my father that he could make good money fast. My father had never left New England. This was a big deal that he couldn't pass it up. My father would be gone for two to three weeks at a time and then come home for a weekend, while we stayed behind with Deborah. We missed him terribly.

Marie and I picked up even more responsibilities on the farm. We fed and watered the animals every morning and evening. I couldn't believe how my life had changed: from going to the Galleria Mall just about every weekend to shoveling shit and lugging bales of hay. We were still responsible for cooking all of the meals and cleaning the house -- that was never going to change. Red did not feel she needed to do anything. We were happy to do our share but this was a bit ridiculous. I know that she had resentment towards my father for leaving her with all of us kids. She started to party with her friends more, leaving us home alone. She even had the nerve to bring two guys and her girlfriend Suzie home with her one night. Suzie and one guy went into the bedroom while Red entertained her friend in the kitchen and then the couples switched. We were told to stay in our rooms and keep our mouths shut. The next afternoon I could tell that Red wanted to say something about what she had done. She told me that they were just smoking pot and she didn't want to do it in front of us. I knew this was a lie. That was something they could have done outside or in their car. Red was not as good a liar as she thought she was. I never told my father about that night. I knew that if I did, that would be the end of a lot of things. Red would be gone. If Red was gone he wouldn't be able to keep us.

When Red was angry, her nickname really fit her. She saw the color red and you knew you were about to get your ass kicked. There were too many ass-kicking's to count but a few stand out. Red loved to slap and punch us in the face. She went for the face and grabbed onto our hair every time. Gobs of hair would be on the floor. Sometimes you could see it coming and other times you had no idea. Marie and I lived our lives walking on eggshells, never knowing what was around the corner.

Somehow, I learned to cope with the anxiety to the point that I didn't even realize that I was anxious. With every experience I had I became stronger. I would climb a hill knowing I would most defiantly be face with another one very soon. I found ways to find peace and calm my mind, body and soul. My escape, even back then, was to go out into the woods. Some things never change. I remember a Sunday evening sitting in the chair watching *Anne of Green Gables* on PBS. I loved that series. I could watch it a hundred times. I would daydream about how I wished I were Anne. I am sure that I had a smile on my face. Red walked by. I was so mesmerized by the show that I didn't look at her. Whenever I watch something that I really like I tend to block out everything around me. She must have thought that I was being a smartass or something because she stopped right in front of me, trying to catch my attention. Red was clearly not happy. She yelled at me, "I know you think you're better than me. I know you think you're special." I had no idea where this was coming from. Out of nowhere, she grabbed onto my hair and threw me down onto the floor. A large mass of my hair was ripped out. I am sure she was high. I just held my head and stared at her. If I yelled back, if I fought back, it would get much worst. It was like riding out a storm. She would eventually get tired and stop raging at me. Red didn't believe in explanations or apologies. She never felt the need to explain her actions, especially to kids. We were beneath her. I still love the *Anne of Green Gables* series. I look forward to watching it uninterrupted with my daughter one day.

There were days that Red hated me and there were days that she loved me. The problem was I never knew which Red I was going to get. Constantly trying not to do anything to instigate a fight was exhausting. Her screaming could be heard all the way down the road. The neighbors would comment on it. They would ask us if everything was ok. It got to the point that I couldn't hold back my sarcasm. I would reply with, "What do you think?" "I'm sure you can figure out who it was," or "The redhead lost her shit again." I had to use humor and sarcasm to hide my pain. My sadness and anger were getting harder to disguise. I could feel it building up. I knew that I was running out of places to put it. I had spent my life swallowing my pain. Even as a young woman I knew this was only a temporary solution to a very serious problem. Sarcasm was working its way into just about everything that came out of my mouth. This did not help my interactions with Red. She was not a fan of smart mouthed girls. When my cup did overflow I would say whatever it was that was burning inside of me knowing dam well I was about to get my ass kicked. Sometimes it was just worth it. I had to get it out. After the beating was over I felt a sense of relief. Sure she kicked my ass, but I was right!

Red was known for her yelling and temper. Her reputation was known miles and miles away. DHHS was called on our family several times. My Aunt Wendy would call. She was worried when she heard the yelling from down the road. We were neighbors, though we lived over a quarter-mile apart. Land in Jackson, Maine was abundant, people were not. Wendy always offered a warm hug whenever we would get the chance to see her. She tried to be friends with Red, but that didn't work out. Red was jealous of her and so we didn't have a lot of opportunities to visit. I thought Aunt Wendy was absolutely beautiful. She would do anything for anyone. She tried her best to keep us safe, but she couldn't. No one could.

My bus driver called DHHS when she saw Red hit me as I got into her car from the bus. She slapped me across the face and grabbed the back of my head forcing my face into the dash, as I got into the car after school, for no apparent reason. This specific time she was upset because I had asked to stay after school to get help with my Science homework. She didn't want us staying after.

"You've got things to do at home," she screamed. "Get your shit done while you're in school and stop trying to make my life difficult!"

I sat in the passenger's seat holding my face and crying. I was crying because of the pain to my face, but I was also crying because I knew that the other kids on that bus just saw me get my ass handed to me. I was embarrassed. If there was ever a doubt in anyone's mind about my home life, it was gone now. Everyone would know by lunchtime the next day at school. I had lost what little control I had. This was devastating to me. DHHS did a brief investigation, but nothing ever came of it. The bus driver would check in on me every once in a while. When she looked at me she looked sad. I wanted to tell her that I was fine. It was mostly my pride that was hurt that day. She wouldn't understand that. What she saw was terrifying to a normal person. To me it was just another hill that I had to get over.

Red had dropped out of school in the ninth grade due to her pregnancy, so she never graduated from high school. I can't even imagine what that life must have been like. High school is so hard under normal circumstances. Many assumptions can be made, but that's all that they are, assumptions. The father of her first child was never spoken of. He did not play any kind of a role in his son's life. I don't know what to even say about this. It makes me sad. It makes me sad for Red and it makes me sad for the father. To have a child as a child is incredibly difficult. I don't know what I would have done if I were put in that situation. I left the projects because I knew that any chance I had of making it would be in Jackson, Maine. I knew about sex. I knew about men. I knew enough to get the hell away from all of it. I feel sad because I don't think she loved herself enough to say "No" and to walk away from something that was hurting her. I think she hated me because she knew I was stronger than she was at that age. This does not mean that I excuse her behavior. It just means that her life was perhaps even more difficult than mine. When thinking of the father my heart hurts. To live a life without your child is a very sad life to live. This is just my opinion, but I know for certain that I could never do such a thing. I say this not because I think I am better. I say this because my heart would be crushed if I could not watch my children grow. That is the type of pain you cannot swallow or hide. It will show in everything that you do.

Red didn't have many friends from what I am told. I know it was hard for her to watch me growing up embracing school and looking forward to my future. I was going to college. Nothing was going to stop me. Everyone knew this. She hated me for it. It wasn't that I thought I was better. I knew I deserved better and I was going to fight for a decent life.

Eventually DHHS required in-home counseling for my family. They had received so many complaints about our situation that it could no longer be ignored or put off. They sent a caseworker to come once a week and meet with us to talk about our "issues." The woman was very sweet. She tried so hard to help my family. The problem was Red was never wrong and my father did not like anyone from the outside coming in and telling them how to raise their kids. The counseling lasted for about a month until my father threw them out of the house. There was no consequence for this. It seemed that as long as our father gave us a roof over our heads and food in our bellies, we were not going to be moved out of our house. We would not tell the caseworker enough to be removed. Again, we knew where that road led and our home was the better option.

Cruel is a word that I do not use lightly. Cruelty towards a child is absolutely unacceptable. It goes against every cell in my body. When you see a child, your first instinct, is compassion. The things that Red did were intentionally hurtful and mean. There was no rational reason for her actions. They were impulsive and brutal at times. Red was cruel. She was evil. She had no business having children or even being around them for that matter.

I have to be careful with these strong emotions when I am at work. There are times when I have to walk away from a situation and catch my breath before I say or do something that could get me into trouble. My partners have figured me out. Especially the ones that have known me for the past 16 years. When there is a case involving child abuse, I tend to gravitate towards comforting the children and settling their nerves rather than dealing with the abuser. With my history, I have to be careful. I am still Irish after all, and my mouth has a way of running away with itself when I am really upset. Thankfully, this is another trait I am learning to control as I "mature." If a situation is too horrific I can manage to block it out for the time being, take care of business, and deal with the emotions, after the fact. I never let anyone see me cry. Anyone, meaning the public. My close friends have seen me cry after a bad case. I am not ashamed of this. It is who I am. I care for the people I help and I would do anything for a child. I think they can tell. If I can calm their crazy little world, even just for a few moments, I will do it. Then we can go from there.

15

Mount View High School 1992-1995

High Schools in Maine are quite a bit different from the schools in Massachusetts.
I always felt safe in this school. It took me a while to fit in, but I always felt safe. We
were poor. The other kids could tell by our clothes. I didn't have a problem with being
poor. I just could never be seen as weak. My pride was strong. I walked with my head
held high. I knew a lot about life on the streets. I could hold my own with my peers. I
knew when to laugh things off and when to fight. Now I had to learn and adapt to life in
the country. This proved to be more challenging than I thought.

Mount View High School, home of the Mustangs, was small and plopped in the middle
of a huge field. It had about 400 students total. Those 400 students came from Waldo
County. Waldo County is a huge county. Most of the kids traveled by bus to school.
The bus rides were long on the winding back roads. Waldo County is a poor county. If
a family had money it was family money passed down from generations of farming.
Land is abundant. The area was beautiful. It was always a pleasant bus ride into
school. Riding the bus was our only option so it was a good thing that we didn't mind
the long ride.

I enjoyed the teachers and staff very much. They were always kind and supportive.
I always wanted to play sports. I had always been athletic. Living over thirty minutes
away from the school playing sports was never really an option. Occasionally I would
be able to try out for a team after begging my father until he would give in. It never

failed that just as I was getting involved Red would pull me for one reason or another. There was never really a rhyme or reason to her actions. After a couple of attempts I stopped trying. I knew I would not be allowed to be a part of any team.

Thinking back to High School, I would never want to go back! Nothing was ever easy for us. Marie and I had lice on more than one occasion, usually after coming back from a visit to see Lori. However, our family didn't have the money to buy the right medicine to treat it. Instead, Red would drench our hair in kerosene and make us sleep in it overnight. She had a grin on her face as she did this. We would be up all night in pain. The burning of our scalp was unbearable. Marie and I would talk through it as we watched the time go by. I remember talking about how much we hated "that bitch". She was evil. This was cruel. If we could just make her sit for two hours with the kerosene in her hair she would get a taste of what she was putting us through. We had to wait until 6 a.m. to wash it out. If we got out of bed before then, we were told we'd have to repeat this treatment all over again the next night. Red got off on this power. It was written all over her face. She was not worried about us. She would make jokes about not going near a flame. We were careful to stay in bed until 6; we knew that if we didn't, Red would make us do it again just because she could. We sat up talking about any and everything. Solving the world's problems. Talking about what we were going to do when we finally got out of this hellhole. I would joke about making Red sit with kerosene in her hair for just a couple hours. She couldn't even make three hours -- never mind the whole night. We would laugh at the thought of this. It gave me a false sense of power. Feeling pride because I could make it through the night with a burning scalp. That's how I survived.

We watched the minutes pass by until finally the clock would say 6 a.m. and then Marie and I would fly down the ladder from our loft and race to the kitchen sink. Since the faucet was broken, we had to rely on a cut-off piece of garden hose. We used pliers to turn the water on and off. We cranked it as fast as we could so that the water rush through our hair as we bent our heads low. The cold water felt amazing! We shampooed several times but the smell would linger for the next few days. A terrible reminder of what had happened. We were helpless. We had huge blisters on the back of our necks and all over our ears and scalp. Some were filled with fluid and some had already popped. The skin would peel off for the next few days. The kids at school would ask what had happened to us. Red would tell us that this was our own damn fault and that we had to deal with it. The feeling of my scalp burning is unlike anything I have ever felt. I thank God I never had to go through that again.

Red only allowed us to shower twice a week, on Sundays and Wednesdays, no matter what our physical condition was. She told us that we dirtied too many towels causing too much laundry. Once, when I explained to Red that I would use one towel a week and that I didn't understand her logic since *I* was the one doing the laundry, it didn't go well. I got a nice smack across the side of my face. I didn't bring that up again.

Showering was not an issue until I hit puberty. That's when my hair became very oily and needed to be washed every day. I looked like a grease monkey. Some days, when it was really bad I would sneak into the locker room before school started and wash my hair in the shower. Most days I didn't have enough time so I would just pull it back tight in a ponytail. Red saw how oily my hair was but she didn't care. She saw that it was causing my face to breakout, too, but she didn't do anything to help. I believe she enjoyed the control, even over the dumbest of things.

Toward the end of my junior year I could feel myself becoming more and more anxious. I had been a stress eater since I had moved to Maine. I had gained about 20 pounds since I had moved to Maine. I could feel this part of my life getting out of control. When I felt anxious I ate. I started to gain even more weight. When I thought of loosing Marie I ate whatever I could find. It became obsessive. I was so worried that my last year of high school was going to be my hardest in that house because Marie would be gone and I would no longer have my backup, my confidant, my biggest fan. I knew it was going to be difficult without her but I had no idea it was going to be as unbearable as it turned out to be. Gaining the weight was the least of my worries.

Before Marie left, Red would sometimes vent her wrath at her, sometimes at me – but never at both of us together. She would have her days or weeklong rants of being pissed at one of us for some reason or another. You never really knew exactly how it had started but you knew enough to shut your mouth and ride the wave. Marie and I always supported each other. If the heat was on me, Marie would step in and help me with my portion of cleaning even if she was exhausted and had homework to do. She would stand next to me at the kitchen sink after Red had emptied all of the cupboards and thrown all of the dishes that we owned in the sink because she had found a spot on a spoon. Overwhelmed and discouraged, I just stood there staring at the dishes. This was also the perfect opportunity for Red to tell me how "FUCKING STUPID" I was and that I was "a waste of sperm." That was one of her favorite lines. She would say that my father should have "jerked off" instead of getting my mother pregnant. Red was classy with her words. Marie always stood by my side. She would put her hand on my shoulder and start helping me with the dishes. We stood there for two hours, washing, drying, and checking for spots on every dish we owned. Wanting to cry but I couldn't give her the satisfaction. Marie and I would just keep going. When Red would turn her back I flipped my middle finger at her and Marie would smirk. That was all I could manage to pull off, but it made us both smile.

As I knew the fall was approaching and Marie would be moving away I became more and more anxious. Even though I was happy for her, I didn't know how I was going to make it alone. Deep down, I wanted Marie to take me with her. So that we both could be free.

Our time together had run out. Marie was off enjoying her freedom. I had to buckle down and get through this year. When I started my senior year at 16 years old, I was the youngest in my class. I was just a kid, but I felt more grown up than all the others. Most of them had no idea the kind of hell I was living with in my home. I would be interested to find out what my classmates knew about me at the time. Perhaps my friends had shared some of my secrets. Perhaps I was not as good at hiding them as I thought.

I do know that my classmates had no idea about my past life in Worcester. It was not something that I spoke about. I was always purposely vague. I only spoke to my close friends, if I talked at all. Something would have to trigger the conversation. I would tell them "my mom has issues." I wouldn't get into the crazy and dangerous things I had seen or lived through. I just couldn't share this part of my life. I didn't want them to know. I wanted to be seen as "normal."

Classmates got glimpses of my Jackson life here and there when Red would come to the school. She was unable to control her mouth. She would swear openly with no respect for the students or staff. Her signature spandex was always loud and obnoxious. She always had to put on a show. I would make a point to tall anyone that was watching she was "my fathers wife." I did not want them to think for one minute that she was my mother. The stories of my life with Red were just too crazy to tell. I knew that even my close friends would think I was making it up. Who would put kerosene in a person's hair? I think they all thought I was just a poor farm girl. It was clear we didn't have a lot of money. I had the bright yellow tickets that showed that I got a free lunch every day. My classmates were cashiers at the local IGA, so they saw me buying groceries with food stamps. None of this bothered me. Again, I was fine with being poor even in this situation. I knew this would not always be my situation. I figured that part was out of my control. What I wasn't fine with was being a punching bag for Red.

Life was never the same after Marie left. There was no one else besides me to take on the brunt of Red's wrath. I told myself that I just had to focus on the finish line. On my graduation from High School. On surviving the next year. I had come too far to break down now. I had worked too hard. I had swallowed too much. I knew what I had to do. I gave myself this pep talk many nights, as I lay alone in my room crying or seething mad. I was going to survive. I was going to "make it" out of poverty and pain. I was going to fight through whatever came my way. I had no other choice.

16

Senior Year - November 1994

Defining Moment #2

The final straw, the final beating, came in late November 1994. This was the second most defining moment of my childhood. I got home around 5 p.m. from a friend's birthday sleepover. It was extremely rare that I was allowed to go to a sleepover but for some reason Red had agreed to let me stay overnight at one of my closest friend's house. Our parents had met several times and my parents knew that it was a very safe place. My friend's father was late returning from work. He was supposed to bring me home for 3 p.m. This caused immediate stress. I knew that Red was not going to be happy and so I was desperate to find a quicker way home. I called my stepbrother, Chris, to give me a ride. I told him I was going to get my ass kicked if I was late. He knew his mother and he knew I was right. He was Red's first child, and was the same age as me. He had been raised by his grandmother, not Red. He was so worried for me, he rolled change he had saved up to get gas to come and get me.

Since we didn't have a home phone, I called my grandmother, Doris, asking her to let my father know that I would be late. I figured that my father would be up at the farm, checking on his cows, and that I could trust my gram to deliver the message. She told me that she had not seen my father but she would let him know. I felt ok about being just a couple hours late especially after making the call. The feeling of comfort only lasted until I walked through the door. I could instantly feel the stress in the air. Everyone was quiet when I walked in. It was like the feeling when you walk into a room and you know that people have been talking about you but they stop right as you walk in. I hate that feeling. I took a deep breath and figured I could just get through the wrath and go to bed. I was not so lucky...

As I walked into the living room, Red snapped, "Get your ass over here!" This was not a good start. She was very angry. My father had not been home and so he never got the message. I told her that I had called and she called me a "fucking lying little bitch". Her eyes were red with anger. I knew what was about to come. She was screaming at me. The spit was flying out of her mouth. "You are an ungrateful little bitch." Flew out of her mouth over and over again. Her face was bright red, her eyes bulging with anger. I couldn't comprehend why she was so angry. This time I was scared, really scared. I was just seven months from graduating. I knew I was almost done. As that thought crossed my mind, I smiled. I didn't realize it but I am sure that I did. I felt comfort in knowing that as soon as I left here, my entire life would change. My smile set Red off and before I knew it I was on the ground. She screamed even louder, pinning my hands back with her knees and punching my face and body until she had no more strength left. Chris and Michael stood by watching. They were scared shitless, I am sure, and didn't know what to do. She pulled wads of hair out of my head as she banged my head against the floor. I don't know how I did it, but I got up. I ran to the door. Red yelled at me to come back. I stopped at the door and screamed back at her in a voice I didn't recognize. I screamed, "FUCK YOU, I AM NEVER COMING BACK!" I didn't...

I ran to my friend Samantha's house. It was exactly two miles down the road. The air was cold but it felt good on my throbbing head and face. I knew that if I went to my grandmother's or my uncle's house I wouldn't be able to get away. I needed to escape. I ran across a field fearful that poachers would be out hunting for deer. My mind was racing and filled with panic. Then almost as if I were in a movie I felt some type of presence with me. A calm presence telling me to keep running. In my heart I know it was my guardian angle. I made it to Samantha's driveway and she came outside, running towards me as soon as she heard my cry. I fell into her arms and I knew I was safe.

Samantha and I had become very close over the past couple of years. She was behind me in school but not in maturity. She carried me inside. My face was soon unrecognizable. Both eyes buttoned up. Huge fat lips. I was a mess. I remember she couldn't look at my face without turning away. I didn't dare look. Her mother Jane and her father Jim told me that I would be safe with them. "We have to take you to the hospital," Jane said. Fearing that at the very least I had a concussion, Jane drove Samantha and me to the closest hospital, which was in Belfast.

Walking into the hospital I didn't have any real expectations. I couldn't hold onto a single thought. I had a hard time focusing when they asked me my name and address. Everything was blurry and confusing. The ER nurse took one look at me and I could see her start to cry. I felt bad because I didn't want her to be upset. She set us up in a room right away and told me that they would be contacting the police. They didn't have a choice. A deputy arrived and I saw him wince when he looked at my face. As I told him what had happened, he wrote everything down in his note pad. Then he photographed my face and body. There was a mirror in the room and when I caught a look at myself. I was shocked. It was the first time I had seen my face since Red beat me. I had bruises everywhere. I could barely see through the swollen eyes. That didn't matter because I couldn't stand to look anyways. I didn't recognize the girl in the mirror. I was in so much pain that I couldn't think straight. I lay down to rest my body.

"You have two choices," the deputy said. "You can either become a ward of the state or you can become emancipated."
I knew what emancipated meant and with just seven months until I graduated I did not want to go into foster care. I was just about to turn 17.

"Your age is in your favor," the deputy added. "You should get a job as soon as you can and make sure that your grades are good. Prove to the state that you are responsible, and not just a kid that doesn't want to listen to her parents."

I knew the officer was right. I had to show the court that I was a survivor!

"She can stay with us," Jane said, and I felt an instant rush of relief.

The deputy was a young man who looked like he had not been on the force very long. He was extremely kind and compassionate. His eyes were sad for me. He put his hand on my shoulder and said, "You're going to be ok," but I want you to promise me that you'll never go back to that house again. You can make it on your own. You're strong and smart, I can tell."

The officer smiled gently at me and made me feel safe. He solidified in my mind that my path in life was law enforcement. I wanted to do for others what he had done for me.

Red was never charged for her assault on me. I found out later that she had said that I attacked her. I know that her sons would not go against her even though they witnessed her holding me down and beating me until she had no strength left. It would be her word against mine. I knew the photographs the deputy had taken would tell the true story. Red did not have a mark on her. If she did, it would have been from me trying to get her off of me. I never punched or struck her in any way. It doesn't really matter now, I got out and that is what I needed more than anything. Everything else would work itself out along the way.

Two days after the incident, my father showed up at Jane and Jim's house and asked if I would come out and talk to him. I was shaking in fear. I was short of breath as the anxiety took over. I was worried that he was going to force me to go back to that house. He didn't know what happened and all he had probably heard was Red's version of her truth. We all knew she was a habitual liar. It didn't matter whom she was talking to. I don't think that she could help herself sometimes. Anyway, knowing this, I was sure there was no possible way that she had told my father the truth. I felt it in my bones but I went out anyway. He would have to look me in the beaten face and tell me that this was my fault.

He sat outside in his blue Buick waiting for me to gather the courage to go out. By this time the swelling had gone down a bit but the bruising was dark. I had two black eyes and a busted lip. My forehead was peppered with bruises as well. My father looked at me and then turned away, his eyes filling with tears. He took a few moments before he could look back at me. I stared down at my hands, playing with my fingernails, waiting for him to speak.

His voice cracked as he looked back at me and attempted to speak. I could see in his face that he was not prepared for this. He felt my pain. He was not prepared to see his daughter, the daughter which whom he shared his name, barely recognizable. He took a couple of very long minutes to collect himself again. My father was a soft soul, and was not one to raise his hand to a child or to anyone for that matter. He was never violent. If he raised his voice you surely must have really pissed him off. He always kept his cool. People knew that if they had a flat tire at 2 a.m., my father was the guy they could call and he would drive an hour each way to come and help them out. When he collected himself he asked me what had happened. I told him from start to finish. To no surprise, that was not the story that he had heard. Red told him that I had attacked her. She was defending herself from his wild and "crazy" 16-year-old daughter. His 16-year-old daughter that never liked her anyway. His "ungrateful daughter."

I stared my father straight in the face. "LOOK AT ME!"

When he did, I said, "Dad, look at my face and think about what she looks like and you tell me to my face that I attacked her. That I beat on her. Look in my bloody eyes and tell me that, dad!!!" He couldn't. He started to cry. I grabbed his hand I told him it wasn't his fault. I felt the uncontrollable need to comfort him. I didn't want him to be sad and I didn't want him to carry the guilt for something that she had done. He asked me what I wanted to do. He told me that I had two options. I could go and live with my mother or I would have to go back to the house. He promised me that this would never happen again. He reminded me that I only had a few months left until graduation. I already knew that this was no longer something we were going to negotiate. I had made my decision. Lori was living in a shelter with Andrew and Jessie. That was not going to be my life. He already knew this. I would never live in Massachusetts again and there was no way I was ever returning to that house again! I told him that I was making a different choice. I was going to be emancipated. I was going to finish out my senior year, in my school, with my friends. I was going to live at Jane and Jim's. I was going to be just two miles down the road but he would probably never see me unless he reached out. At this point I was solid as I spoke. He knew that there was nothing else he could say that would change my mind.

Before I could get out of his car I had to ask him a question. I had to ask him how he could stay. "How could you go back to that house and look that woman in the face like everything was ok?" He told me that it wasn't going to just be ok. He said that he was very upset and she would know what I had told him. The house would never be the same but then he continued with explaining that he still had a young son with her. He was still responsible for him. Red was his mother and he couldn't lose him, too. He said that I would be gone soon anyway and if he broke it off with Red he would probably never see his son. This pissed me off. I felt instant rage as he spoke, but I knew he was right and so I gave him a hug, told him I loved him and then got out of the car. I walked into the house and broke down in tears. Thankfully, I had Samantha and her family there to support me. When I needed space they gave it to me. When I needed love they gave it to me. When I needed encouragement they gave that to me, too. I was blessed and I knew it.

By the end of the week I had a job at the IGA. I walked in and asked to speak with the owner. I still had bruising and one black eye. I promised the owner Gary that I would work harder than anyone else that he had working for him. The first week I was stocking shelves, within a month I was working in the kitchen. My work ethic paid off. I took whatever hours I could get. Starting off with a "kid I will give you a shot" and 12 hours a week. Gary knew my situation. I think everyone in town did. By the second month, I had 30 hours a week. My grades went through the roof. I could study without distractions. All of my stress was gone. I felt like a new person. Everything was better! I looked better; I started to slim down a bit. I stopped with the stress eating. I always thought my over eating was because we never had food when I was younger. My close friends all know this. When the shit hits the fan hide the salt and vinegar chips from me!

With my new freedom came some pleasant surprises. I started to dress and feel like a girl. My waist was becoming defined. I started to exercise whenever I could. Ending my senior year I went on my first "real" date, followed by a few others. Unfortunately, I couldn't commit to anyone because I knew as soon as that bell rang and I was handed my diploma, this girl was leaving Jackson and never looking back. I did break a few hearts but it was never intentional. I would do stupid things to purposely make boys go the other way when I thought they started to like me too much. I felt awful but I did not want complicated. I had enough of complicated, for a while at least.

My senior year flew by. I saved up most of my money, only splurging on a few clothing items. When I left my dad's I left with the clothes on my back. I didn't care and just a month later I had enough money to buy what I needed. People noticed too. At school classmates would ask me where I got the new clothes. I never had new clothes. I just told them that I got them for Christmas. I was happy that not many people in my school knew about my beating. It had happened at the beginning of Thanksgiving break. By the time I got back to school I just had one eye that still had blood in it and slight bruising. A little makeup and it was almost unnoticeable. If they did know they were kind enough not to talk about it. One of my teachers mentioned my bloodshot eye in front of the whole class. I just laughed and said I had been screwing around and fell. She didn't go further. By the end of the week all of my teachers knew what had happened. They were asked to keep an eye on me because I had been through a terrible ordeal and had moved. I could see the compassion in their faces when they looked at me. We never spoke of it. I was just told to let them know if I needed anything, including extra time to get my work done. I refused to do this. My batteries were charged and I was ready to get things done! There was no reason to milk my situation for special treatment. I never wanted anyone to see me as a victim or as weak. I wanted to be seen as a person that could take it on and beat it. Mission accomplished!!! Since the county was so large it helped with disguising my secret from the other students. Life was not like the projects, where if the police came to your door, at least 100 people were watching through their windows or outside in the courtyard. I do appreciate this part of rural living! I later found out that the nurse that treated me had a daughter in my class. She and I never spoke of the incident but when I saw her I could tell that she knew. I was grateful that she kept my secret and let me live out my senior year on my terms and not as a victim.

I graduated in June of 1995. Two weeks later I was at the University of Maine in Orono for a summer program called Upward Bound. I took my English 101 course that summer. I also had a job at the campus police department set up by the program. It was more like an internship. I got to get an inside look at law enforcement while hanging out with the officers. This was a blast and they paid me to do it! The officers spent one on one time with me. I was able to spend hours driving around in the police cars. I organized some of their offices to stay busy. I loved being around the officers. They were happy to share their stories and offer me insight to the world of law enforcement. I could see myself working amongst them in the future. They saw something in me too. The eager little beaver that wanted to be just like them. I knew they were happy to have me around. Once again, I felt extremely blessed.

That fall I started the Criminal Justice program at Southern Maine Community College. I was dropped off with a black garbage bag with everything that I owned inside. I also had 64 dollars in food stamps. Those were the last food stamps I would ever have to use. I was determined to support myself. I walked into the entrance of my dorm with my garbage bag and I was so proud of how far I had come. I did not flinch at carrying the black bag. This was who I was and dammit I was on my way. The fact that all I owned was in this plastic bag showed just how strong I was. I walked it up the four flights of stairs and located my room. I put down the sheets and an old bedspread that Jane had given me. I sat on the bed in the place that would be my home for the next year and I couldn't stop smiling. There was no going back for this girl and nothing in my way!

The Criminal Justice program was a two-year associate program. I flew through it, the youngest in my class. My classmates took me under their wings. The teachers went out of their way to look after me, too. I shared small portions of my story along the way. I never got too deep, but just skimmed the edges enough for people to know that I was on my own. In class, there were sometimes discussions that would resonate with me personally, particularly when we spoke about emancipation or drug use and addiction. I was clearly the best person to explain these systems and the laws around them. I lived through them. By the end of my second year, I was confident my instructors believed in me. They managed to figure me out over the two years. I was glad that they did. It strengthened my desire to join law enforcement so that I could help others. I considered my teachers close friends. We stayed in touch for many years.

Holiday breaks were a little nerve-racking when people would ask where I was going. I was blessed to have some amazing friends and their families welcomed me with open arms. They knew that I didn't have anywhere to go for the holiday. They knew that I had booked shifts on both ends of the actual holiday finding myself without family around or a home to stop in to. Jackson was a long drive for one day. I shared just enough about my past to help them understand me but without revealing too many

scars. I never wanted that! I couldn't handle it and honestly, I was embarrassed. But

that's not the case any longer. I would go back to Samantha's when I had more than

one day off. I took as many hours as I could get and if that meant staying in Portland

during holiday breaks then so be it.

My new friends and some other kind people taught me how to drive and helped me get

my driver's license. The kids in the dorms knew that I didn't have a license. They

wanted to help me. They took turns taking me out driving. I had a driver's education

team. I had at least four different people willing to take me on the back roads in South

Portland. We parallel parked in the school lots. With such a large team I was able to

get in plenty of practice. I had my license in just a few short months. I took the test in

Portland. Passing my first time. I had three jobs by the second month of my freshman

year and that never changed. I worked day and night. When I didn't have a ride home

in the middle of the winter, I didn't care -- I just walked back. The kids with cars felt

sorry for me some nights when they couldn't give me a ride. I never felt sorry for

myself. I took one day at time working towards my goals. I loved the feeling of having

my own money. I was never going to want or need for anything ever again.

I have always been really good at stretching a buck. I saved up and bought my first car

in the spring of 1996. No cosigner needed. I had saved enough money to make a

decent down payment. I lacked experience in negotiating the purchase of a car and so I

paid too much for my 1993 red Ford Escort. It took me about a week to realize that I

had been screwed but honestly I didn't care. I knew I would never make that mistake again -- and besides, I finally had a car. I could go wherever I wanted to, whenever I wanted to. If I wanted an Italian at ten at night, which I often did, I could drive downtown and grab one. I was very much in love with my newfound freedom.

The weekend after I bought my car, I drove it to Jackson and surprised everyone. I did not go to my father's house but I knew he would hear that I had been up, and that I had bought a car on my own. I believed that deep down he would be proud. I still wanted to please him even after he hurt me. Even after he walked away. I still loved him. I would just need some time before we could talk again.

It was over a year before we spoke. It was four years before I would pull into that driveway. I went in a few times to visit with my father but I never felt right. I would always prepare myself for how I was going to feel after. I made a point to stop in when Red's car was not there. I had no interest in talking with her. I was there to visit my father. Our conversations were always surface talk. He would ask how I was doing in school. He would ask about my work. I would tell him a few silly stories of things I had seen or done. Our visits were pleasant but the conversations were very safe. He always sat in his old stained blue cloth chair. I sat across from him on the beaten down couch. I only talked about the things that wouldn't create a serious conversation. Neither one of us wanted that. He wanted to know that I was doing well and happy. I wanted to know that he still loved me. After my visit I would need a day or two to collect myself and to process how I felt. That house was hell to me. If I could burn it down, I would.

I transferred to the University of Southern Maine in 1997. I toggled between the University of Southern Maine and Southern Maine Community College, adding classes working towards my BA. In that year I was hired by the Ogunquit Police Department at the age of 19. I was trained in their 100-hour Reserve Officer program. The training took place in the same building as the Ogunquit Police Department. A representative from Ogunquit PD came into our class to let everyone know that they were looking for additional summer help. I was very nervous about applying. I thought I was too young and that they probably wouldn't hire me. Lucky for me, that was not the case. I had a one-hour interview with the patrol sergeant and the next day I learned that I had been hired. It was a 40-hour a week summer position. The pay was the best that I had ever earned. There was also potential for work during the winter months if I did well. I knew that this was the beginning of my career in law enforcement.

I was told that I would be spending that summer walking the Marginal Way in Ogunquit. At the time I had no idea what that was. Now I know that the Marginal Way is definitely one of the most magnificent places I have ever seen. It is a walking trail that is just over 1 mile long. It runs along the coastline. The view is spectacular! Every time you make a corner you find yourself with a new breathtaking view of the ocean and beaches. The waves pull your attention as they crash up against the rocks during the high tide. There really is no place I would rather be than the Marginal Way and I have traveled the world. It was the perfect place for me especially as I began this new chapter in my life. My main responsibility was to patrol the ocean walk and talk with the tourists. I was absolutely perfect for this job. Since my independence day, I couldn't stop looking for new adventures. I couldn't stop traveling. I would take road trips to any place that sounded interesting. I would save up and work overtime to book a trip to whatever warm place I could find a good deal to visit. I loved experiencing life and I loved meeting new people. A million pounds of weight had been lifted and there was nothing stopping me from a deep belly laugh and feeling happiness. I chose life and I chose to love myself. It would have been very easy to be angry and bitter. I remember thinking that the only thing it would do is make me look old. How did I have this insight at such a young age? Good question.

Life just kept getting better at this point. Someone was clearly looking out for me. After my first year in Ogunquit I landed a housesitting job in a 2+-million-dollar house on the Marginal Way. I found a small classified ad in the local paper looking for a house sitter. The location of the house was not listed. I figured I had nothing to lose so I would just give it a shot. A week later I sat down with the owner for an interview for the position of house sitter. After about an hour, she looked at me and said I was exactly who they were looking for. This woman had more money than anyone I had ever known and she said that "I WAS EXACTLY WHAT SHE WAS LOOKING FOR." I felt that I was living a dream. I went from living in the projects to living in a small mansion on the ocean for free. I lived there for two years, and worked as many hours as possible so that I could pay off my student loans within those two years. That Escort was paid off as well. I managed to save fourteen thousand dollars to put towards the purchase of my first home. Every week on payday, I would proudly walk to the Key Bank in downtown Ogunquit and deposit no less than $200 into a savings account that was just for my future home. Some months I deposited $800 but if I worked a lot of overtime I could manage to put double that amount. I was determined to save for my own home. The teller was so used to me coming in that as I walked up to the counter, she would always ask, "House fund, Jamie?" and I would say, "Yes ma'am!" with a big smile on my face.

The Marginal was an absolute gift to my life. I would wake early in the morning to run along the ocean. I was getting fit and feeling amazing. I have nothing but great memories from this time in my life. I felt amazing inside. I can honestly say, during these years I began to put myself first and I was kind, both to myself and to others. I grew into an adult living in that house. I had been on my own for a while but just getting by. Now I was making progress and moving ahead. Nothing was standing in my way. Great things were in my future I could feel them.

I never invited my father or my mother to the beautiful house on the Marginal way. I didn't want to share it with them. I don't know why I felt this way. At this point in my life I had been communicating with both of them on a regular basis. Still, I didn't want to share. Marie would visit. She would spend a few days appreciating everything around her. We would go for long walks and enjoy everything that Ogunquit has to offer. As for my parents, they were not welcome.

Years have past and lives have changed. After having my own children I no longer felt the need to return to my past. I began to build my own life with my own children. I would talk with my father occasionally on the phone. My children knew who he was but had a very distant relationship with him. We lived a couple of hours away and life is crazy with small children. This is what I told myself. I would make the drive once a year to check in with everyone. I never felt at home when we went. It was also important to me to shelter my children from that part of my life. My father was a very sweet grandfather. He never forgot a birthday and always wanted to know what sport or activity the kids were into. He wanted to be a part of our lives. As these years past our relationship started to grow again and the past was left in the past.

Red died almost two years ago. She was only 50 years old. Her lifestyle caught up to her, and her body simply could not handle the amount of substances she was putting into it. I attended her funeral to support my father. I stood in the back with Marie. We had support of some close friends. They were there to support us, not Red. My father was more important to me than the hurt I still carried from Red. The rain fell as we listened to the minister speak about Red's love for her family and friends. I laughed to my self. I knew most of the people at the service and they knew me. They knew my history with Red. They knew that she beat on me regularly. They knew about her demons. I would get a glance here and there. The words that I wanted to speak would only hurt my father. I could not do that to him. Not on this day. Not ever. I would never intentionally hurt my father. I knew he would live out the rest of his days thinking of his wife as his love taken too soon. I had to leave it alone. I had to move forward and leave Red behind in that grave. I did not return to the house after the service. I did not have anything to say at the time. It took me a couple of weeks to process how I felt about her death. I was sad that my father would be alone, but I was also happy for him. I knew that his home would be peaceful for the first time in a long time. The screaming and fighting had finally stopped. I hoped that he would be able to quiet his mind and

144

relax. It took him a few weeks to adjust but eventually he did. He was calmer when we spoke on the phone. I could see positive changes happening for him. I was happy for him. He was becoming the father I knew as a young child. I loved my father with all that I had.

Now, it's 20 years since the night I made my escape and I know I will never return to that house again. My father passed away just over three months ago. I held his hand as he took his last breath. I spoke to him fighting back tears, telling him it would be ok, that we would be ok. Marie was across from me but unable to speak. Her pain overtook her at this point. I wanted to console her, too. This was the hardest thing I have ever done. I spoke to God and begged for it to stop. I felt as if my insides were being ripped out. I had never felt that kind of pain. I knew God could hear me. I could feel him. I had to keep talking to my father and I couldn't leave his side no matter how bad it hurt. This ripped my heart out. I pray I never have to feel that type of pain again...

As I sit here writing this part of my story I realize that today is his birthday. March 22nd. He would have been 60. He lost his life to lung cancer. He was too young to die. I wish he could have read this book. He had no idea about my personal struggles in the projects. He knew about my mother but not in any great detail. We never told him most of what had happened to us. He didn't need to know. It would not have changed a thing and it would have only made him sad. I do believe that my father regretted his life choices back when he was 22 years old. I know that he didn't want us to live in the projects but he also knew that it was no longer his choice to make. When he would drop us off with our mother after our summer vacations with him, he would always cry

as we said goodbye. As he drove away I watched him wipe his tears. He loved us and

I forgive him.

18

1998

York Police Department

All of my hard work paid off when I was hired by the York Police Department.

I was just 20 years old when I landed my first real job with benefits. I was absolutely overwhelmed with excitement and joy! I interviewed with four other applicants and was one of two hired at the York Police Department as a Communications Specialist. I was the youngest in the group. By the youngest, I mean, by at least eight years. I had done some dispatching in Ogunquit and so I was familiar with the position. However, I still had a lot to learn considering Ogunquit is a four-square-mile town famous for its amazing beaches and social diversity. York was a very different animal. It was similar to Ogunquit in appeal but it was spread out over 60 square miles and had a much larger population. I went from a dispatch center that was just busy during the hot summer days to a center that was hectic year round. The York dispatch center was expanding and they were putting two people on per shift to cover the extra workload. York was also taking over Ogunquit's communications so we would be dispatching for both communities. I was now making more money at one job than I was at my previous three. I was excited to only have to work at one place now and overtime was available every week. Life could not have been better for this money-hungry girl!

Training for this position was harder than I thought it would be. It took me a while to get it all. Communications has many moving parts. The position requires a lot of multitasking, especially during an emergency. At times it was very stressful and I needed to build up my own sense of confidence. I would also need to get the required certifications. Since York is such a large community, I began learning the layout of the town as quickly as possible. I drove around the town in my car during my free time to learn the roads.

I loved the fast pace of the job; multitasking constantly so that the shifts would fly by. My co-workers were all very supportive and encouraging. They took their time to train me even when I thought I already knew it all. I definitely had to be put in my place a few times, rightly so, and I respected them even more for doing it. I had to keep my Massachusetts attitude in check. I no longer had to defend myself. I would catch myself saying "this is bullshit!" When the training felt overboard. I soon realized they were there to help me. It was clear to me right off why no one ever left York Police Department. It wasn't just a PD, it was a family!

There was no secret that my life goal was to be a police officer. When I interviewed for the communications job I was very clear about my long-term goals. I wasn't sure if I would be hired in York as an officer at first. The officers there are extremely smart, motivated, educated, and physically fit. I knew that I would need to really get my rear physically in shape and start studying. I read every book I could. I read the books I kept from college on criminal law. I read any book remotely related to beginning a career in law enforcement. I wanted my brain to be sharp. I knew that reading constantly would only help me think fast and clearly. I analyzed what the officers were doing and how they handled their cases. I took the things I liked and put them in the back of my head and I rejected the traits I didn't care for. This was so interesting to me.

The officers were every make and model. Some would stop a bunch of cars and make lots of arrest. They spent their shifts looking for violations. Other Officers, the community focused officers would walk around Short Sands Beach and hang out with the shop owners and kids. I knew I wanted to be a happy medium in these areas. I also knew that I wanted to be around kids more than anything else. Every community needs a nice balance of both. Police departments need officers that hit traffic hard to slow down the speeders and keep our streets safe. They also need officers that can sit down and talk to anyone, to make them feel safe and comfortable even if they have spent their whole life has been fighting against authority. We had it all. I knew York was the place for me. I just didn't know if I would ever get the chance to show them all I was capable of doing.

Just over a year after I was hired, there were two openings for patrol officers. I had worked full time in dispatch and I also picked up extra hours working as a reserve officer in the beach square for extra money and experience. I applied for the job and I was ready for it. I had started running and shed 15 pounds right off the bat. I continued to read every book I could get my hands on. I rode along with the full time guys to have that experience under my belt as well. I was ready, or so I thought.

It was time to take the tests. The room was filled with candidates. The written test was first on the list. Everyone looked the same, clean cut, bright-eyed, and wearing dress clothes. I don't recall any other females but I am sure there was at least one. As they handed out the test, my heart was beating out of my chest. My hands were sweaty. I started to second-guess myself. I asked myself if I was good enough, smart enough, and did I even deserve this job? What if they found out about my past, my mother, and everything I had stolen? What would they think about my past? It would all come out. Was I ready for that? I had worked so hard to get there. This was my dream. I couldn't stop thinking about all of the bad things that would come out. I stared at the pages on the test but couldn't read. I would answer a few and then stop. Then a few more and then stop. I looked around and everyone was focusing hard. Finally, I gave up and started just filling in circles. I couldn't think straight. I handed in my test, which they corrected immediately. I knew I had failed. I walked away acting as if I was fine but inside I was absolutely devastated.

When I returned to work, everyone knew that I had failed. I was happy to hear that two of my friends had passed and were on the right track to get the jobs. They did end up getting hired and still work with me today. I believe that this happened for a reason and that this was their day and mine would come soon after.

Six months later, we had another opening. I would not be letting this one get past me. I studied day and night. I had booked and paid for a solo trip to Bermuda and I cut it short to make sure I was available to get *my* job. I scored high on the written test without a single hesitation. I had the number-one score in both my oral board and my civilian board interview. I nailed the chief's interview as well. I was unstoppable. That is, until I had to fill out the background check information. I had to tell the detective about my mother and how she was currently living in a shelter for drug addicts. I had to tell him that I was emancipated when I was 16 and the story of that night. He would need to go and visit with my family members so this was very important information. I told them about my history of thefts. I told them everything, all of my little secrets. The things I never shared would need to come out. I couldn't risk them finding out about my past any other way. I was petrified about what they would think or say to me, but my Lieutenant at the time, who is now my chief, just said "We all have a past kid. It's what you do with your future that matters to me." I will never forget it and if I had not been so nervous I would have hugged him right then. He had my back and I will never forget that. I will be loyal to my chief until the day I die. He gave me my chance and I promised that I would never let him down.

The Academy was long and hard. I left on January 3, 2000. We did push-ups in the snow at 2 a.m. We ran until we couldn't take another step. We stood at attention, starving and waiting for permission to eat. The yelling never bothered me. I had learned how to tune that out a long time ago. The structure didn't bother me. I was used to asking *how high* when someone told me to jump. I thrived in the Academy. My cadre told me that they never worried about me. The cadre are seasoned officers responsible for our training in the Academy. They knew I was a fighter and that I would make it through. When I started, I had bronchitis but I didn't complain once. They said that they knew right away that I was a fighter. Everyone knew that I was sick since I was coughing constantly and I sounded like a seal in pain. When they asked me if I was ok, my only reply was "Yes, sir," with a big smile on my face. Today, I wouldn't volunteer to go back, but I also wouldn't change going for anything in the world. I call that type of training "character building." I think by now I have enough character.

After the Academy, I had 12 weeks of field training. It is a very strict training program where a new officer works one-on-one with a training officer. You are evaluated every day on everything you do. This program is designed to prepare you for being on your own, and to make sure you are mentally and physically equipped to handle yourself no matter what the circumstance.

It was very stressful. I knew I would be working a lot of nights and so it was very important that I knew what I was doing. My FTO (Field Training Officer), in my opinion, was the hardest in the bunch. He would never stop! He was constantly asking me questions and quizzing me while I was driving the car and trying to look for violations. I probably told him over a hundred times (in my head of course) to *shut up please!* I prayed he would stop so I could have a single thought go through my head at a time. He was trying to frazzle me. I learned how to pause and think, buying myself time to come up with a decent answer. When I tried to bullshit him he always called me out on it. The worst day of my training was a day that started at 8 a.m. and did not end until the next morning at 3:30 a.m., when he finally told me to go home. Even worse, I was due back in at 8 a.m. to work in our detective unit. I was a mess!!! I scored high for that day but was absolutely no good for the detectives. I came back at 8 a.m. and by 10 a.m. they sent me home. I was told to sleep for a while but then study my laws and be prepared for the next day. I never complained about the long hours or the stress I was under. I was so grateful to be there that I would do whatever they said. My gift for gab came in handy. I talked down the angry six-foot drunks and cheered-up the crying kids that were scared for whatever reason that brought me to their home. I knew I was right where I needed to be, and that I would not want to be a police officer anywhere else. York PD was my home and my family now.

I have a confession to make at this point in my story. After finishing my training and passing all of the required tests, there was one more thing I needed to do – for myself. I had to make a call about something that had been bothering me since I was seven or eight years old. I had to let someone from my past know what I was doing with my life. It was one of those things, as adults, we say are not necessary. To prove someone wrong is catty. But I needed to be catty. When I was young and living in the projects, there was a woman that lived in apartment A, right across the hall, with her two young sons, Andy and Frankie. Her name was Misty Small. I will never forget her. She was a single mother working hard to get herself and her boys out of the projects. She was putting herself through nursing school. Misty allowed me to hang out with the boys in their apartment, and since Andy and I were the same age, we became good friends. I loved Andy and Frankie. One day, Andy and I were sitting on the front steps to our building playing some game -- I don't remember the game, but I do recall it was a warm, sunny day. No one else was around, which was unusual in the projects. People were always running around. Andy suddenly stopped what he was doing and just looked at me. He paused for a minute as if he was unsure if he should say what was on his mind. Then it came, like a punch in the face, but worse. Andy explained to me that he was told by his mother not to get too close to me. Misty told him that they were leaving the projects soon. She also told him that I was going to end up a prostitute. She said that my life would be spent sleeping with men for money. Andy and I both knew what a prostitute was. Living in the projects, unfortunately, you grow up too fast. I can't imagine what possessed her to say this about me to her young son. I don't know why Andy felt the need to tell me this very hurtful thing. To his mind, I guess he felt he was telling me the truth. He was sad when he spoke. I remember watching his lip quiver. He didn't want me to be a prostitute. He was worried about me. I said that I wasn't upset with him, but I was hurt by his mother. I also promised him that I would not be a prostitute. I told him that I would do something important with my life. And so after my training was completed and I knew that I was an official police officer, I called Andy Small and I told him about my new career. I told him that I was very happy. He asked if we could get together some time. I told him that I had a lot going on but I asked him to do me a favor and tell his mother about our conversation and give her my best. I never spoke to Andy again. I needed to make that call for myself and for the little boy that was once my friend.

19

2015 - Full Circle

I am 37 now and as I look back over the past 16-plus years since I started at York Police Department, I realize I have had many moments where I felt my life has come full circle. I have a strong belief that everything happens for a reason, that I am here for a reason, and that my life has a purpose. With all the things that have happened to me, I am convinced that I had a destined path. It can be as simple as meeting a person and feeling as if I have known them forever or walking into a room or building and knowing that something was going to happen. Some full-circle moments are created by us as well. It starts with an overwhelming urge to develop an experience. We decide that we want to make something happen because of an experience that we had and it usually works out. Where there is passion and will there is always a way!!!! I never forget where I came from and I look forward to where I am going.

The clearest full-circle moment for me occurred when I became a DARE Officer. I grew up surrounded by drugs and alcohol. It destroyed many of the people in my life. They all made choices, I get that, but substance abuse destroys lives. It destroys the users and it can also destroy the innocent victims, their children, and other family members that want nothing more than to love them. The new DARE curriculum is focused on decision-making. Teaching our youth how their choices have consequences and rewards. As a city kid, I went to the DARE fair at the Worcester Centrum because it was a free event that offered us a special fun- filled day. A group of us would take the city bus in. They had bounce houses, balloons, and goody bags. My goody bag had a DARE ruler and pencil along with some stickers. To me this was the best present ever!!! It stood for something that I believed in even back then. Now, I hand out those stickers and pencils. I light up a little face with a simple sticker that is shaped like a badge. I can see how it makes a young person's day. I do believe that I am right where I am supposed to be. If only I never had to work patrol again I would probably do this for the rest of my life. Unfortunately, that is not the case. My position requires that I work in the car during our busy summer months. As I get older I find myself dreading the nights in the patrol cars dealing with all of the things that come along with the night shifts. I am past the days when patrol filled me with excitement.

That being said, I truly believe that from that day of the DARE fair to the day I started as the DARE officer, I came full circle. At the time I had no idea that I would be a DARE officer. Life has a funny way of working out.

Some full-circle moments are put into motion without our knowledge; others make them happen. These next few stories are full-circle moments that I created and even though the way some of them turned out broke my heart, I wouldn't change a thing about any of them! You will understand what I mean.

While working as a communications specialist, I decided that I wanted to give back. I wanted to mentor a young girl that perhaps had a difficult home life. I thought, *Who better to do this than me?* I had a big sister for a short while growing up and I still remember going to her college dorm and playing Frisbee. I went to the York Middle School, which is where my office is today, and met with a counselor that ran the mentor program at the time. I told her of my interest in mentoring and explained a small bit about my past. When I asked if she had anyone that may have a similar type of home life to the one I had, her face lit up right away and she said, "I have just the girl." This girl was living with her grandmother because her mother had died and her father was nowhere to be found. The girl had struggles with physical and sexual abuse at a very young age. She didn't have any positive role models. She certainly did not have a great view of police. She agreed to give me a shot.

I started by visiting her once a week at school. We would play simple board games like Checkers or Connect Four. I would bring lunch so that she could have something special. Every week, I would ask her what she wanted for the next week. This made her very happy. I know that she looked forward to our lunches. I realized quickly that she didn't have a very large wardrobe. She often wore the same clothes. I knew how this felt and I knew how kids could be about this kind of thing. I bought her clothes several times. I didn't have anyone to spend my money on anyway and it was great to see her in nice clothes. She was always very appreciative. After about a year, I was able to pick her up at her house and bring her to mine for a visit. I was living on the Marginal Way so this was a treat for her. We would go for a walk. I made sure to explain to her that this was not my house. I told her that I was very lucky to live here and it was only because I had worked hard and earned the owner's trust that I was able to live in such a fantastic house. As we would walk we would talk about boys in her class and sometimes we would talk about her family. We made cookies and acted silly more often than not. She would talk to me about the other family members that lived in her grandmother's house, and how they struggled with substance abuse. Too many people lived in that house. They were stacked up one on top of another. When I went into the house there would be dog feces on the floor and dirty dishes piled up on the sink. The house smelled like filth. I couldn't stand it. It brought back too many memories for me. I knew how much I could take and this was too much. She always wanted to show me her room but it got to the point that I asked my friend to just meet me outside her house.

Years passed and as my friend got older she started to act out in school more and more. As much as I tried to change her life I was just a small part of it. I got a call from my partner while I was away for training, letting me know that there was an assault investigation going on with my friend. She was 12 years old and she was pregnant. I remember sitting on the bed in my hotel room and uncontrollably crying. My partner apologized to me on the phone but said he thought I should know sooner rather than later. I cried for her. I cried for me. I cried for that baby.

My friend and I lost touch quickly after it became public that she was pregnant. She had managed to hide the pregnancy until the last stage of her pregnancy. Soon after, she had the baby and he was raised by another family member. I bought her baby clothes and the essentials for a newborn and dropped them off at the house. I did this a few times as I knew she would be struggling. We never spoke of the deliveries. She returned to school but we were no longer working together. When she came to the high school, I was working as the resource officer. She battled with self-harm. She would sit on the nurse's bench and rip her hair out with her own hands. This bench was just five feet from my office entrance. I couldn't stand by and watch her hurt herself. When I tried to stop her, she punched me. Suddenly, I was in a physical altercation with a young girl that I cared for deeply. This broke my heart. I had all I could do to hold her back. I couldn't look at her as a criminal. I couldn't look at her as the enemy. All I could see was the little girl that I use to bake cookies with. She fought me for about ten minutes until my partner came. She was put into restraints and taken into custody. She went to the hospital to be evaluated and I went home. We never spoke again. I often wonder what happened to her. She moved away. I believe she had more children. I hope she is happy doing whatever it is she has chosen for her life.

Working in the high school I had more than one opportunity to help young people struggling with their issues. I was also able to see that there was poverty in York, Maine. There were kids that didn't have enough money for a winter coat or decent boots. York has every dynamic. I see single moms struggle, juggling two jobs to try to pay their rent to keep their kids in the school district. I don't blame them one bit. I remember sitting at my desk and thinking that I needed to do more. I needed to reach out to these less fortunate families. I thought about one Christmas when we lived in the projects and we literally had no gifts. Not a single present. We didn't have a tree, Christmas lights, nothing! Lori had told us that she didn't have any money and that she would make it up to us. My father had not sent a package that year either.

On that Christmas morning, we heard someone knock at the door. As Lori answered it, Marie and I were standing right behind her. There was a tall woman with long brown hair. I remember thinking how beautiful she was. Beside her was a man with a black peacoat. The woman handed my mother a large black trash bag and said gently, "We thought you could use these. Someone told us you may be having a tough year."

Lori was nervous and shaking. I prayed she would take the bag. She did and then handed it to us. Marie and I ran into the living room and dumped everything that was in the bag on the floor. I couldn't believe all the toys that tumbled out! I don't know how my mother ended that conversation but I was so happy. We spread out the toys, separating the ones that were for Andrew and Jessie from the ones for us. Then we took turns picking. One for you and one for me until they were all gone. My first gift was a Yahtzee game. This started a tradition. Marie and I played Yahtzee every Christmas Eve and Christmas that we were together. That was the best Christmas ever! Until I had children of my own that is.

I decided that I wanted to give back to the families of York. I met with my chief and pitch my idea. He loved it. I told him that I would work on getting the donations and let him know as I made progress. I had a lot of help from the support staff in the office as well as other officers. I could not have done it without them. The program has helped many families. We buy winter jackets, boots, clothing, and diapers -- basically anything someone may need. Basic needs are always met. We also try to give each child one wish. A gift that they have been asking for but their parents probably can't afford. We have been doing this program now for over ten years. We help between 20 and 30 families each year. I would love to let that woman with the long brown hair know that I took her gift and paid it forward. Who knows? Maybe she will read this book.

After I had my son Jack, I thought about how much different his life was going to be from mine. I thought about how he was going to be able to experience so much more as a child than I ever did, and this made me very proud. It also made me think about those students in my school that, even though they live in York, Maine, would be spending their summer sitting on their couches. They did not have anyone encouraging them to get out and play. I knew of kids who had lived in York their whole lives but had never been in a kayak. York has miles of beaches. It also has a couple of wonderful pond areas perfect for getting into a kayak. I was 23 the first time I sat in a kayak, and I loved it so much I went out and bought one of my own. I wanted to give that experience to my students. I also knew of students that had never hiked Mt. Agamenticus. It's a small mountain in York with perfect trails that lead up to the top, which has a spectacular view. I thought to myself, *How can anyone live in York and never set foot on Mt. A?* So I had an idea. I wanted to start a summer camp for young teens. I would find sponsors so that it would be a free, daytime camp. I envisioned that there would be three parts to the camp day: The first would be time for a workout. I wanted to get those kids off of the couch and moving. The second part would be classroom time, where I would teach them about basic criminal laws, have a panel of guest speakers, and talk about decision-making. The third would be a couple of hours of community service. I would show them how to give back. I also wanted to make sure that they spent some time with some of our seniors in the Senior Center. I thought it was important that they connect with our seniors and I knew our seniors would get a kick out of connecting with them. I wanted them to see that not all teenagers are a "pain in the ass."

It actually worked! The kids and the seniors had a blast playing Wii bowling and chess. Each summer, the seniors would ask us to come back. We also held a free car wash for them. All they had to do was pull up and we would wash their cars. Unfortunately, the camp lasted only four years. The economy was in rough shape and it was hard to find sponsors. We were also short-staffed and some patrol officers didn't understand why I was able to "get paid" while kayaking. I wish they had come to me directly. I would have explained that the kids in my camp would never have had a chance to go kayaking if it were not for the camp. I was just a bonus. I'm glad this camp gave a lot of children memories to cherish for a lifetime. I have wanted for everything during my life and I wouldn't change that! Because of that experience, I appreciate everything that I have now. Seeing those kids enjoy themselves filled me with happiness. As I get older, I am truly learning to take things one day at a time.

Empowerment is an incredible gift. Young women especially deserve to feel strong and deserve to feel safe. One day, as I was sitting with my dear friend and partner at the police station, Evan. I mentioned that we were lacking in one area: our girls had no opportunity to learn how to protect themselves unless their parents made the investment to pay for expensive self-defense classes for them. I figured that since we were a police force and safety was our number-one concern, it shouldn't be too difficult for us to convince my chief that we had a need. He was always supportive.

I found a program that could be offered with very minimal cost, if any. The biggest expense was our time, and Evan and I were more than happy to work that out. The program we wanted to teach was called the RAD (Rape Aggression Defense) self-defense course. This is a nationally recognized program for women. Evan was married and had three daughters and he was invested in the program as much as I was. It was important to both of us. We were committed to doing whatever it took to bring this program to York and to communities in the York area. We would not turn anyone away.

Evan and I approached the chief and pitched our idea. He smiled and said, "I support this 100 percent." He loved the idea. He was raising a daughter as well, and he recognized the need and our passion for this program. Evan and I got into the next certification class. It was held at the Portland Police Department and it was not a walk in the park. The stress level was high. The instructors took their teaching very seriously. This was not your typical police training. We were used to a 15-minute bullshitting break every 45 minutes followed by an hour-long lunch and all of the coffee and snacks we could want. These instructors meant business. I was actually intimidated by the head instructor. Her name was Lori and I thought for sure she could kick my ass. I figured she was a former police officer (if she wasn't, she should have been). Her passion was profound. She wanted this program to flow through all of our communities and to help as many women as possible. As a result of her passion and intensity, I felt empowered. I would soon have this gift to give to other women. It was a gift for my family and I, but it was also a special for anyone that I could find to take the course. I recognized the gift right away and I appreciated it.

After receiving our certification, Evan and I got to work right away. We put out a press release. We posted classes in the Adult Education flyer. We could now add to our resumes that we were self- defense instructors. We would teach women of all shapes and sizes how to have strength and power. No one was too old and you did not have to be wonder woman to take this course. We would work with any dynamic.

Over time, I noticed a pattern: our first class in the series of four sessions would usually be filled with 15 to 30 women. They would sit quietly and listen to our lessons. Their voices would be nervous as they asked questions. I could see they were all wondering how this was going to work. Most of our students had never punched anything in their lives. This seemed strange to me, of course, but this was their reality. There was always one student in the room that had the face of someone who had been through something traumatic. I couldn't tell exactly what had happened but it was serious enough for her to seek out this course. There was a fire in her eyes, and there was hurt as well. I could feel her pain as she punched the bag. Each time she punched or kicked or yelled "NO," I felt her get stronger. I could feel her spirit growing. As I watched her learn to stand up for herself, I took in the emotion emanating from her. When others first entered the room, they used jokes to try to break the ice or calm their nerves. Not this woman. For her, it was game on and she was in it to win. Every time I saw a woman like that, I would tell her, "You're a survivor. You're going to make it."

The class ended with a night of scenarios. The women fought off up to three bad guys, each wearing the big red padded suit to protect them from being hurt during the training. By this time they had practiced their skills and they were ready to defend themselves. This was my favorite moment in the program. The cheers filled the room as the bad guys went down, but more than that I could see that their hearts were filled. They were filled with pride, strength, and courage. This was our gift to them and they knew it. I never felt burdened by RAD, even though I had to balance this class with being a mom and working my regular duties. I always managed to fit RAD into my schedule because I knew it was the right thing to do. We continue to teach this program in York. I have a new team of instructors and our goal is to have every young girl in our school district take this course before their graduation.

Finally, I sit here today having experienced a full-circle moment just a couple of hours ago. I have a fifth- grade fitness/gym class I teach twice a week. Due to the forward-thinking of my school's administration, which developed this course, I have been teaching the students for a year. The class has nothing to do with law enforcement. I focus on building their confidence with physical exercise while having a lot of fun! I try to think of something different for each class. Today, we had an obstacle course that was absolutely hilarious, followed by a game of boundary ball. I wanted to play, of course, since it was boys against girls; I had as much fun as the students! I want them to look back on this class when they are older and not be able to stop themselves from smiling. How many cops let you hit them with a ball and then chase you down wanting payback? When my students think of police officers, their first memories will be of me and that fills my heart!

20

2014

DARE

In the spring of 2014, I was approached by my sergeant asking if I would be interested in taking on the DARE/SRO position at the York Middle School. I had been at the high school for just about eight years and I was extremely comfortable there. I compare it to sitting on the couch in a cozy, broken-in spot with your favorite throw blanket and having someone asking you to move your seat. My first reaction was "no thanks!" The officer leaving the position had been there for over 20 years. I knew that he worked very hard and that the program at the middle school was phenomenal only because he made it that way. I didn't want to leave my comfy office or try to fill his shoes. As time went on, the position remained vacant and it was clear that my bosses were struggling to find the right fit for the position. I knew that they had wanted me to take it. I also knew that I would be tripling my workload. I would now have to work out of three schools instead of one. This meant taking on a lot of extra projects that the community had come to know and love. The DARE officer before me had worked very hard to create a successful program. I knew I would have my work cut out for me trying to fill those shoes. Deep down I was ready for the challenge. There was a very powerful force in my corner. I love children and children love me. My house is the house that the kids come running to when they want to play. I am the mom doing cartwheels on the front lawn with all of the girls. I am energized by them and so I knew that the relationship part of the position would be a natural fit. I was born to be a "kid cop." There was no doubting that. It was the rest of responsibilities that scared me.

It took me about a month to decide to take the position. I was both excited and nervous about the new challenge. I had so much to learn and a short time to learn it. The DARE certification school was a two-week course. I had heard that the program was extremely stressful and the expectations were set very high right from the start. I realized it was all or nothing and so I decided to go all in. I met with my chief and sergeant and let them know that I was willing to take on the position. I was immediately signed up for the certification course for two weeks during the summer. I started at York Middle School the first week of September 2014.

The position has been extremely challenging. It is difficult to come into a school that has had the same officer for over 20 years and expect everyone to open to a new approach. This was not my house. Fortunately, the staff has welcomed me with open arms. I can be honest in saying I don't know if I would have stayed had they not. It is supposed to be all about the kids but if I couldn't work well with the staff, then I couldn't do my job effectively. I have changed a few things and left a few things the same. Change is good I keep telling everyone, including myself.

As for the little people, I could not be happier with their reactions to me. I enjoy every second that I have with them. They look at me as if I am a superhero. It's hilarious. Most days, I go out of my way to make them smile because I want them to be left with a warm heart and a huge smile. I need for them to trust me in order to do my job but I also need them to see me, the *real me*, in order to keep their trust as they get older and life happens to them.

I am extremely happy that I decided to teach DARE. I believe in the new curriculum 100 percent. I use a lot of what I have learned with my own children. Life is about making choices. Our choices have either positive or negative consequences. Most importantly, we all have a responsibility to ourselves and to other to behave in a safe, kind, and compassionate manner. Everyone has their own story, which is precious to them. We all need to respect each other's situations and demonstrate kindness and understanding to those in difficult situations. That is the message I will bring to my students as long as I am their DARE Officer.

21

Crisis – Lessons Learned

When someone is making bad choices due to circumstances in their lives that are so very overwhelming that they need an escape, I refer to that as being "in crisis." I believe I have been "in crisis" more than my share. When this happens, I tend to go into survival mode. I shut things out of my head, I compartmentalize them so that I can cope with everyday life stressors and circumstances. As I have been writing this book, more and more memories have come flooding back. Most of them are traumatic and extremely painful. I wonder how I made it through so many challenges with a head that seems to be screwed on straight. Well most days, that is! I believe my defenses told me to lock those harmful events away because I would not be able to move forward if I didn't. It would have been easy for me to be a victim, or to be angry at the world, or to try to escape my pain with drugs and alcohol. I chose to do better for myself and for my family. I chose my own path. To this day I still have situations that are so overwhelming, that I have to put them away. I struggle with child abuse cases. I need a few weeks to process through them. It is hard for me not to reflect on my own experiences when I am helping someone in a similar situation. I know this about myself and so I set myself up for success. I talk more about how I am feeling close friends. Police officers typically don't talk about their feelings. We are supposed to be able to handle anything. I would not be able to continue my journey in law enforcement if I tried to swallow my feelings. They don't go as far away anymore. I pull them out when I am ready to and break them down piece by piece. I still screw up. I will never be perfect and, frankly, I am more than ok with that. I wouldn't be a good police officer if I were perfect. I wouldn't be able to relate to people. Imperfection is a gift!

Yoga was recommended to me by a very dear friend when I was in crisis. I was in the middle of my divorce. Being a very uncoordinated individual I did not think yoga was going to go well. I was wrong. It was exactly what I needed. It taught me how to breathe through anxiety and how to get back my focus. I would never call myself a natural at it but I held my own. This steered me to calming teas and relaxation instead of medications and alcohol. I do not believe in self-medicating. I have seen too many times the damage it can do. This friend also gave me a few very helpful books that seemed to be exactly what I needed to read at the time. I read one book three times, and I still crack it open on occasion when I need a little reality check. It's called *A Return to Love* by Marianne Williamson, and it helped me find my focus on so many different occasions. Each time I opened the book, it seemed I turned to the exact page that I needed at that moment in time. I truly believe I was meant to read that book. I have recommended it to so many of my friends dealing with similar situations.

From the outside looking in, I see people in crisis at my work just about every day. Some know that they are in crisis but most have no idea. Their head is spinning so fast that they lie and tell themselves that they are in control. They make poor choices not because they want to but because they are not thinking clearly. I get it! Their anxiety is at a ten and they can't seem to slow themselves down. They are not sleeping and it shows on their face and body. Their brain is racing like a hamster on a wheel. You cannot think clearly or make sound decisions when you're not sleeping.

Having been in crisis more than my share, I have the ability to recognize it almost immediately. This is not what I consider a gift but more of a learned ability. I can also recognize when someone needs help or if they just have to figure things out the "hard way." Like watching a car go off the road, you know you can't stop it from happening, but you can't seem to look away. Even though you know it is going to be terrible you continue to watch. Whenever I see someone who is clearly in crisis, I always recommend that they slow down. I ask them to take a few steps away from whatever entanglements are contributing to their crisis. Clarity will come if they take a few deep breaths and calm their body. I also tell them not to make any decisions in the heat of the moment. It's always helpful for me to write things down and give myself a few days to sift through things. I have one additional piece of advice: *put down the phone!* We have all been taken over by our devices. We are so engulfed in social media and instant responses and impulsivity that we never slow down or disconnect. When we are in crisis we are not thinking clearly and when we are not thinking clearly we tend to post or text things that we would never normally post or text. We make bad choices, as the DARE teacher inside of me would say. We need to reconnect with ourselves before we can reconnect with anyone else.

22

Motherhood and Law Enforcement: The Best Part of My Life

For as long as I have known that I wanted to be a police officer I have also known that I wanted to be a mother. As a nurturing person, who loves little ones, I always knew that I wanted children of my own. In April 2005 I was married and in March of 2006 my first child was born. My son Jack was born three weeks early, weighing six pounds even and my life has never been the same. People with children know that your entire world is suddenly thrown upside down. Other parents try to help by telling you stories but you are never really prepared for what is in store. Jack changed the way I looked at everything.

When I returned to work I was on evenings, doing ten-hour shifts that lasted until 2 a.m. I nursed Jack the first year of his life, and this is no easy task for a woman wearing a bulletproof vest every day. I would pump in the basement bathroom of the police station. The guy's locker room is attached to this room and they could hear the pump. It didn't really bother me. Most of them were dads and completely understood what I was doing. The young hires got a quick lesson thanks to my partners. I just laughed about it. It was for Jack and so I didn't care. I had mastitis at least two times. The vest did not accommodate letting things flow.

My position at the high school had been filled by another officer when I left for maternity leave. As I patiently waited for the position to be open again, I worked patrol and juggled being a mother, a wife, and an officer. My husband at the time was just hired by the Maine State Police. This was a very big commitment for our family. We all did the best that we could. His schedule was extremely difficult. Worse than this was the parental pull that I felt. I could no longer go to work and not worry about getting hurt. It was always in the back of my mind. If something were to happen to me, what would happen to Jack? This was the least favorite part of my job. There was not a single shift that I didn't worry. I could feel myself becoming anxious, and I knew that I had to figure out a way to handle that stress without allowing it to take over. I was petrified that I was going to hesitate when action was needed. Hesitation is the worst mistake an officer can make.

I started to slow everything down. I took a few deep breaths to help me think clearer. The old Jamie would run into a house without waiting for her backup and "get shit done." The new Jamie slowed everything down. I would purposely slow my breathing down when responding code three to a call in order to try to control my heart rate and adrenaline. Code three is traveling with lights and sirens operating in order to get through traffic quickly. We only use this code during serious emergencies. I wanted to think clearly. I wanted to evaluate and process each scene a little better now in hopes that I would never get hurt. I knew that I needed to take in the whole picture rather than run through the door just after convincing myself that I had it all under control. When you're 22 and right out of the academy you think you are invincible. When you are 28 and have a child at home you know that you most definitely are not.

Just over a year after I returned to work, my position at York High School opened up again and I jumped at that opportunity. That following September I was back in my office, working 7 a.m. to 3 p.m. and I couldn't have been happier. I would tell my colleagues they could throw anything at me all day long as long as I am home at night with my family.

In August of 2008, my second child was born. She was absolutely stunning. Riley stole all of our hearts immediately! I was able to keep my position at the high school this time and so when I returned to work the transition was not as difficult. Riley was an easy baby for the first few months. She slept like a dream. We thought we had it made. But that changed when Riley was about five months old. She struggled with acid reflux and would scream whenever we tried to feed her any kind of food. It took a while, but with the help of doctors we were able to figure out the issue. Some medications helped and others made it worse. Once we were able to get in to see a specialist at Maine Medical Center things started to get better. Up until this point I was operating on three to four hours of broken sleep a night. I was absolutely worn out and useless on most days. Thankfully, everything calmed down and the sleepless nights of walking Riley up and down the hall were over by the time she turned one year old. The amount of relief that I felt was absolutely incredible. I was able to nurse Riley for a year as well. Now that I was in the high school, my options for pumping were wide open. Eliminating the stress of a uniform was absolutely priceless. Life seemed easier as a working mom with two than it had been with just one. I am sure that is because I knew what to expect this time and I thought I had everything under control.

When Riley was a one year old, I realized that divorce was most likely in my future. Things were not good at home. My husband and I were working opposite shifts and the stress of our jobs became wearing on each of us in different ways. I was overwhelmed with all of the duties at work and at home. My husband was never home and if he was, the stress level was at a ten. Our relationship was a constant roller coaster. I felt as if I was always on edge. All that I wanted was a happy and healthy home. The relationship became toxic and so it ended.

Fast forward to today: Jack and Riley are both doing very well. Fortunately, their father and I found a way to put their interest in front of our own and protected them from the residual effects of a nasty divorce. We co-parent and the kids have settled in well with both of us. This is no small task, as any divorced parent knows. A lot of children I work with from divorced families struggle for years. Unfortunately, egos and hurt feelings can creep in and without realizing it parents are hurting their children in the name of revenge, hurt, and pain. On many occasions I have had to remind parents that we are all meeting together to discuss their child and not their relationship with their ex-spouse. My ex and I are not perfect by any means, but I am grateful that we have both focused on putting our children first.

Jack is nine now and loves football and playing with his friends. Riley is six and I call her my "mini me." I look at her and I see my face. I look into her eyes and I see love, joy, and kindness. I have no doubt that both Jack and Riley will do great things with their lives. I hope they find something that makes them happy and will grow up to help others, even in the smallest of ways. I take them with me to work when I can in hopes that some of it wears off on them. I want them to feel the compassion that I feel. I want them to crave some type of public service. I want them to want to give back. Their journey is their own and I will support them wherever that road takes them. I also promise to be honest with them and share my knowledge of this world in hopes that they will always surround themselves with kindness and love. If there is a function, fundraiser, or special event, I make sure that they feel they are a part of this. I have so many opportunities to impact my students, and I feel the need to make sure I impact my own children as well.

My students love to cling to Jack and Riley. It makes my children feel special knowing that my students have all heard their names and know little bits about them. While helping out at my annual DARE basketball tournament, a group of fifth-grade girls got excited figuring out that Jack was my son. His reaction was priceless. He simply stated, "I know you guys think my mom is special BUT to me she is just my mom..." This cracked me up. It filled my heart with joy. He had the biggest smile on his face and I could see that he was proud that I was his mother. I was a superstar that day and I will never forget that. I also make sure to tell them about any charity events that I am working on. One of the best gifts that I can give them is compassion and kindness. I want them to feel compassion for those less fortunate and be kind enough to help when they can. Riley has seen me writing this book. She asks to read it. I told her she could when she is 30. I'm joking, of course, but I will make them wait until they are adults and can handle finding out the struggles that I went through. I know that this will not be easy for either one of them. Since I began writing, Riley has decided that she would like to be a writer as well and has since written at least three small books. This just shows me that it is not what we say that matters the most but what we do.

23

Collateral Damage

I realize that I would not be true to this story if I didn't take a long hard look in the mirror at my life today. I always tell my partners that I have my job covered. I feel confident and I have "got this." I will admit that I look to the younger officers to keep me up to speed with the changes in laws and our policies and procedures. I am not afraid to ask for help, especially when I have been primarily working in the schools for ten months and then transferred into a patrol car for the busy summer tourist season. I have always said that a great leader is a person that can recognize his or her own weaknesses and appreciate others whom are strong in those same areas. I do not have a problem asking a patrolman in his 20s how to do something. I try to give back in return and help the younger officers any way that I can.

Just the other day a close friend said to me, "God, Jamie you are so strong." I replied, "Thank you" in a low voice, but inside I heard the words *if you only knew.* I do not see myself as strong. I do not feel that I have my "shit together" as they tell me. Some days I wonder, *is this the day they will figure it out? Is this the day that the people around me, will see who I really am, as if my soul was standing there, exposed?* So many people have hurt me. So many nights I have wondered if I would really be ok. Over the years, I have managed to quiet these voices. They are still here --just not as loud and not as often. This, too, is part of my journey.

I am obsessive about exercising. I have gotten better about this in the past couple of years but for me it is my release. I try to slow myself down and walk some days instead of running. I still do Yoga. I still get caught up thinking those things take too long and I have too much to do. I am absolutely terrified of commitment. Any kind of commitment gives me instant anxiety. I do a risk assessment on basically everything that I do or touch. I have the bumper plates up. I overanalyze everything. The worst side effect is my lack of trust.

Trust they say is something that is earned. You build it up as your relationship grows. I don't trust anyone. I guess it makes sense since I could never trust my mother or my father. How am I supposed to trust anyone when I couldn't trust in them that they would keep me safe and make the right decisions for me? People lie to me on a daily basis. When I am working and trying to help them maneuver through a difficult situation they continue to lie. This was something that took some getting used to. In my job, people instinctively lie to me because they don't want to get into trouble. The only time they come around and tell me the truth is when they know that I know what really happened. The little white lies and the big lies are all the same. People say what they think that you want to hear. You can tell when this is happening but we ignore it most times because we don't want to create an uncomfortable situation over something that doesn't really matter. People lie to one another in front of us and we again stand by because it is not any of our business or it's just not worth it. We lie to ourselves. We tell ourselves that everything is ok or going to be when deep down we know that it is most definitely not ok. Trust is such a precious thing but it is often discarded for personal gain. It's as simple as someone talking garbage behind another's back. It happens every day in our line of work or really any line of work. Because this happens, I feel like I can never really heal or trust anyone. I am always waiting for someone to hurt me, I wait for that phone to ring, for some person to blow up my entire world with a few short sentences. I am not sure if I will ever change. I have to believe it will. I know I will always do my very best.

I love the people closest to me with all of my heart. I will do anything for a friend in need. I handpick my friends very carefully. The people that are close to me are there for a reason. I can count my closest of friends on one hand. They know who they are, and they know me inside and out. I love them with everything that I have. I want to be able to trust them completely. I just don't know how to do it. Perhaps that's what my next book will be about...

24

Forgiveness

Most of the terrible things that have happened to me occurred before I was 17 years old. That was 20 years ago. I have not been able to find forgiveness for the people that hurt Marie and me in the most terrible of ways. That forgiveness is going to be a long process. However, I have been able to move forward with my life. When I moved away and started my own life I began to heal. I have forgiven my mother. I know deep down she did not hurt us intentionally. She has no skills. She has no "tools in her toolbox," as I say in trainings. I carry hurt feelings and sadness, but never hatred or ill will. I will continue to move forward. This book is brutally honest. That's just who I am. I will always tell you the truth. It may not always be eloquent, but it will always be the truth.

I have read books about finding inner peace and forgiveness. They have helped to soften the trauma that I suffered. They have helped in processing and forgiving myself for some poor choices that I have made over the years. My goal is not to "let it go." My goal is to learn from the experiences and teach others how to deal with their own demons. We all have a story and each story is special to that person's journey. I have been asked about finding forgiveness for those that hurt me as a child. I cannot forgive anyone that would hurt a child. There is nothing more precious in this world than an innocent child. I will fight for those children. That is my truth. That is my drive. That is all that I have. What happened to those that hurt children is on them. On their hands. One day they will have to answer for their actions, if they have not already.

As I come to the close of this book I am filled with emotions. When I started writing I wasn't sure that I would ever finish. I have always felt a pull to share my story, my life, and my struggles so that it will help others who are struggling. Life is hard. Good people have bad things happen to them. All that we have is our spirit and our drive. Pushing forward is all that I could do. The alternative was not an option.

My life has been a complete rollercoaster of heartbreak and joy. I hope that you will find inspiration in this story. If you are struggling, remember that you deserve better and that only you can make the changes you need to make. Don't count on wishing, count on yourself! FIGHT!!! Everyone has a story. Everyone has struggles. You can always find someone worse off than you are. In helping others, I have helped myself to heal. In sharing my most private secrets I have to believe that it will pull someone out of their pain and inspire them to get up and make life happen. There is always risk in stepping out of our comfort zone. There is always fear in wondering what people will think. Judgment has no place in my life. I tell my students to surround themselves with people that make them feel good inside. It's as simple as that. Just remember that it will not happen overnight. Change takes hard work and determination. If I can do it, anyone can.

Moving forward I have to focus on my family's future. I cannot wait to go on my next adventure.